THE PICTORIAL HISTORY OF
RAILWAYS

THE PICTORIAL HISTORY OF
RAILWAYS

JOHN WESTWOOD

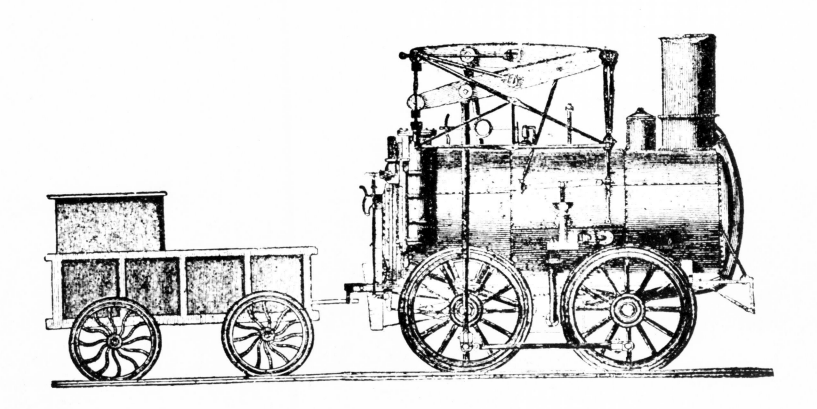

Bison Books

First published in 1988 by
Bison Books Ltd
176 Old Brompton Road
London SW5 0BA
England

ISBN 0-86124-446-X

Printed in Spain

Page 1: The *Cumbrian Mountain Express*, pulled by an 'A4' Pacific, at work in the
north of England.

Page 2: The Canadian Pacific Railway's *The Canadian* travels alongside the Bow
River, east of Lake Louise, Alberta.

Page 3: The *Stourbridge Lion*; the first full-scale locomotive to run on a United
States railroad.

Pages 4-5: A scene on the meter-gauge, privately owned Rhatian Railway in
Switzerland.

CONTENTS

PART 1

THE EARLY YEARS

The First Steam Railways

It would be wrong to describe northeastern England as the birthplace of the railway, for its 2 essential components, the railed way and the mechanical traction running over it, first appeared elsewhere. Wooden rail-ways were used for horse traction in European mines at least as early as the sixteenth century. In North America an early railroad appeared in the eighteenth century; a short cable-operated line was built by British troops at Lewistown, New York, to move supplies uphill from the Niagara River to their base. Early in the next century, the 3-mile Granite Railway was built at Charlestown in Massachusetts, and this had an iron strip that formed a running surface on top of the rails made of wood.

The first successful railway steam locomotive was the Cornishman Richard Trevithick's 1804 creation, which ran on an iron plateway in South Wales. It was also in South Wales that the first regular movement of railway passengers took place; over the horse-operated line between Swansea and Mumbles in 1807.

All the same, if northeastern England cannot claim to be the birthplace of railways, it can be described as their cradle. For it was here that lines built variously of wood and of iron, of rails or L-shaped plates, linking mine with wharf, gradually progressed to a point where steam traction became not only practical, but also greatly preferred.

At the Middleton Colliery Railway, near Leeds, John Blenkinsop introduced 2 steam locomotives in 1811 whose cylinders drove pinion wheels that engaged in projections cast on the side of 1 rail. They could pull 150 tons at 3mph, and among the many mechanics who came to view them was George Stephenson, enginewright at Killingworth Colliery.

Not far from Killingworth, at Wylam, William Hedley proved

Stockton & Darlington Railway.

The Company's COACH

CALLED THE

EXPERIMENT,

Which commenced Travelling on MONDAY; the 10th of OCTOBER, 1825, will continue to run from *Darlington* to *Stockton*, and from *Stockton* to *Darlington* every Day, [Sunday's excepted] setting off from the DEPOT at each place, at the times specified as under. (*viz.*):---

ON MONDAY,

From Stockton at half-past 7 in the Morning, and will reach Darlington about half-past 9; the Coach will set off from the latter place on its return at 3 in the Afternoon, and reach Stockton about 5.

TUESDAY,

From Stockton at 3 in the Afternoon, and will reach Darlington about 5.

On the following Days, viz.:---

WEDNESDAY, THURSDAY & FRIDAY,

From Darlington at half-past 7 in the Morning, and will reach Stockton about half-past 9; the Coach will set off from the latter place on its return at 3 in the Afternoon, and reach Darlington about 5.

SATURDAY,

From Darlington at 1 in the Afternoon, and will reach Stockton about 3.

Passengers to pay 1s. each, and will be allowed a Package of not exceeding 14lb. all above that weight to pay at the rate of 2d. per Stone extra. Carriage of small Parcels 3d. each. The Company will not be accountable for Parcels of above £5. Value, unless paid for as such.

Mr RICHARD PICKERSGILL at his Office in Commercial Street, Darlington; and Mr TULLY at Stockton, will for the present receive any Parcels and Book Passengers.

M. APPLETON, PRINTER DARLINGTON.

Previous spread: Although this photograph was made on the London, Chatham and Dover Railway, it may be regarded as a representative British scene for almost the entire steam era. Inside-cylinder 6-wheeler locomotives, like this late nineteenth-century example, were the favorite type for general freight work in Britain.

Above left: The poster advertising the Stockton and Darlington Railway's passenger service and, like much else on the early railways, imitating the style of the road-coach industry.

Left: George Stephenson's original steam locomotive, built for the Hetton Colliery in 1822. The photograph dates from the 1920s, after the locomotive had been preserved as a relic.

Above: Predecessor of the steam railway, a scene on the Derby Canal Tramway, one of many British horse plateways built for short-distance freight and using L-shaped iron plates and flangeless wheels.

Right: Trevithick's third and last locomotive in London. For a short period the engine earned money as a novelty attraction, giving the public a chance to ride behind it at one shilling a go.

that iron wheels could grip iron rails without resorting to cogs and pinions. Hedley's locomotive was also scrutinized by Stephenson, who built his own steam locomotive in 1814, which was very similar to Blenkinsop's but without the cogs. It could pull 50 tons at 3mph, replaced 20 horses, and was soon joined by other engines of similar type.

The Hetton Colliery Railway, opened in 1822, was not only powered by Stephenson's locomotives but was also surveyed and constructed by him. When it was decided to build a far more ambitious 25-mile railway from the river at Stockton to the collieries around Darlington, Stephenson's reputation gained him appointment as the new railway's engineer. The Stockton and Darlington Railway (S & D), although essentially a long colliery line, also carried miscellaneous freight and passenger traffic in scheduled services, making it the genuine precursor of the modern public, or common-carrier railway.

The S & D Railway was laid with 2 types of track because the directors had been unable to choose between cast iron and wrought iron. All the rails were of the fish-bellied type, deeper in the middle than at the ends, and were seated in cast-iron chairs. The chairs were pinned to wooden blocks cut from the oak timbers of warships made redundant by the ending of the Napoleonic Wars, although at the Darlington end, blocks made of stone were used.

Stationary engines drew the trains by cable up 2 inclines, but steam locomotives were used for freight trains on the long level section. These were built at a new locomotive works which Stephenson and his son Robert had established at Newcastle. The first of the initial 4, *Locomotion No 1*, hauled the long inaugural train on 27 September 1825. Carrying over 500 pas-

Right: Hetton Colliery in the 1820s, showing the steam railway in use.

Below: The first locomotive to work on a public steam railway, *Locomotion* of the Stockton and Darlington Railway. The photograph shows the engine exhibited on a plinth, from which it was later removed in favor of preservation under cover. Built by Timothy Hackworth, it shows the solid construction favored by that mechanic. The transmission of thrust from the vertical cylinders is by rocking arm and connecting rod.

Below right: A scene at the Rainhill locomotive trials, with the victorious *Rocket* in the foreground. Behind is Hackworth's entry, and in the background, the Ericsson creation. The *Rocket* is drawn quite accurately, and shows the direct drive from the inclined cylinders.

Overleaf: The triumphant inauguration of the Stockton and Darlington Railway. Many more than the invited guests turned up to ride the train, but the most honored visitors secured a place in the solitary passenger coach *Experiment*. A horseman with the red warning flag can be discerned a few yards ahead of *Locomotion*.

S. & D. R. N° I. 1825.

OPENING OF STOCKTON AND DARLINGTON RAILWAY

1825 FROM A SKETCH BY THE ARTIST.

sengers instead of the expected 300, and incurring only 2 brief breakdowns and the amputation of a brakeman's leg en route, *Locomotion No 1* reached 15mph on 2 downhill stretches.

The Stephenson firm, Robert Stephenson and Company, soon developed a healthy locomotive-building business, founded on its success with the S & D Railway. Among its early exports was the *America*, a 4-wheeler built for the Delaware and Hudson Canal Company, which needed steam railroads for its coal mines in Pennsylvania. Together with the *Stourbridge Lion*, built by another British company, the *America* arrived in the United States in January 1829 but seems to have remained unused. The *Stourbridge Lion*, on the other hand, made a spectacular trial trip but was too heavy for the flimsy track and saw no further service. Although a small steam locomotive built by John Stevens had already circulated on an oval trial track at Hoboken, New Jersey, the *Stourbridge Lion* was the first full-scale locomotive to run on a United States railroad.

Whereas the *Stourbridge Lion* slightly improved upon Hedley's second colliery engine, *Puffing Billy*, the *America* was a development of the more modern *Locomotion No 1*. Locomotive design progressed rapidly in the late 1820s. Timothy Hackworth, superintendent of the S & D locomotive stock, developed the blastpipe, which passed exhaust steam up the chimney in such a way as to provide a draft for the fire. The Stephensons introduced the 6-wheeler with their *Experiment*, built for S & D freight service, and with their *Lancashire Witch* they brought the cylinders down, inclining them at 45 degrees; this reduced the damaging up-and-down thrust experienced by the previous vertical-cylinder designs, and also made springing of both axles into a practical proposition.

Meanwhile George Stephenson had been appointed consult-

ing engineer to the Liverpool and Manchester Railway (L & M), whose directors could not decide whether to use locomotive or cable traction. To help them reach a decision, the pro-locomotive faction suggested a locomotive competition over a portion of completed track at Rainhill. This took place with the enormous publicity that the British traditionally accord any unusual sporting event. There were 3 serious competitors. Stephenson entered his famous *Rocket*, which was a *Lancashire Witch* with its connecting rods removed (that is, it was a 2-2-0 rather than an 0-4-0). It was also noteworthy for its multi-tubular boiler; instead of passing the smoke and hot gas from the fire through a wide flue and up the chimney, Stephenson provided twenty-five 3-inch copper tubes leading from the firebox, through the waterspace of the boiler and from there up the chimney. This was a borrowed idea, but the execution was novel in its precision, and the innovation raised more steam for the same expenditure of coke. Another competitor, *Novelty*, designed largely by the same John Ericsson who would design the ironclad *Monitor* in the American Civil War, was ingenious but lacked robustness; during the competition it disappeared in a cloud of sparks and smoke when its leather bellows caught fire. A more serious rival was Timothy Hackworth's *Sanspareil*, based on his powerful *Royal George*, built for the S & D Railway. This performed fairly well until several manufacturing defects put it out of the running, so the *Rocket* won. The real prize was not the monetary award, but the subsequent flow of locomotive orders, not only from the Liverpool and Manchester Railway, but from a host of other new companies which were appearing both in Britain and overseas. During the Rainhill trials the *Rocket*, weighing little more than 4 tons, hauled 13 tons and reached the unprecedented speed of 29mph. This was bad news for coach proprietors.

Early Intercity Lines

Being the first intercity railway, the Liverpool and Manchester Railway proceeded on a basis of trial and error, evolving methods and techniques that subsequently became standard on British railways and, to a large degree, on overseas railways too. For example, the L & M's refusal to guarantee arrival times was perpetuated on all subsequent railways of the world. On the other hand, the total ban on smoking was soon changed, as was the regulation that policemen pursuing a criminal could travel free but were required to pay the correct fare if they caught him.

As with subsequent railways, the L & M, although initially aimed at freight traffic, soon gave priority to passengers. Freight trains had to wait in a loop or siding to allow passenger trains to overtake them, and they had no fixed schedules. At first, fires caused by locomotive sparks were a hazard on freight trains, and so open cars were covered with tarpaulins; a practice which continued on British railways for more than a century afterward.

Early passenger services followed the traditions of highway coaches. Lineside coaching inns sometimes became railway booking offices, and buying a ticket was a long process in which details like dates and times and seat numbers, as well as names and addresses of passengers, were laboriously handwritten on the paper ticket. As highway coaches had 'outside' as well as 'inside' passengers, it is unsurprising that some preferred to travel on the sides and roofs of rail vehicles, and many passengers fell or collided with bridges until the practice was totally banned.

The L & M was officially opened in the presence of the prime minister, the Duke of Wellington, on 15 September 1830. During the festivities the *Rocket* ran down and fatally injured the President of the Board of Trade, Huskisson but, despite this, the day was considered a success. Although freight traffic developed

more slowly than had been hoped, passenger traffic was unexpectedly large. After just 6 months the Company was able to announce a dividend, and by summer 1836, 12 passenger trains were running in each direction, of which 2 were first class, making the 31-mile trip in 1 hour and 20 minutes.

Even before it was opened, the L & M Railway received delegations and engineers from railway committees of other cities. They typically visited the L & M and the S & D and then returned home to write up their recommendations. In 1828 2 engineers came from Baltimore, which was planning to lay a railroad to the Ohio River to win back traffic lost to other American ports. The men took back encouraging ideas, as well as a conviction that the British gauge of 4 feet 8 inches (later stretched by ½ an inch) should also be adopted for American railroads.

Nevertheless, the Baltimore and Ohio (B & O) directors still believed in the merits of horse traction, and when the first 13 miles to Elicott's Mills were opened in May 1830, only horses were employed. It was the enthusiasm of Peter Cooper, a New Yorker who persuaded the directors to allow him to try out his small vertical-boilered locomotive, that changed this situation; *Tom Thumb* may have lost that famous race against a horse, but

Above left: An 1873 aquatint showing the Middleton Colliery, with one of Blenkinsop's locomotives at work. The center wheel is the cogwheel.

Above right: Early freight cars of the Baltimore and Ohio Railroad. As in Britain, much freight traveled in open cars, sheltered by a tarpaulin.

Right: A Baltimore and Ohio Railroad vertical-boiler locomotive of 1836, remodeled for exhibition purposes to resemble an 1832 design. The rear 2 vehicles exemplify the influence of road-coach design on early railroad passenger cars.

A CARRIAGE OF THE FIRST CLASS
L & M RLY. 1838.

Left: A Liverpool and Manchester Railway first-class vehicle of 1838. The buffers are evidence of technical progress, while the rooftop seat is an echo of coaching practice.

Below left: A contemporary print showing a variety of early locomotives and rolling stock of the Liverpool and Manchester Railway in 1831. The clear distinction between first class (upper train) and third class (second train) is well shown.

Below right: An 1893 working replica of the Mohawk and Hudson Railroad's *De Witt Clinton.* The original locomotive also exists, but is inoperable.

only because of a slipped belt, and its demonstrated convenience and speed caused the directors to think again. Horses had been rented from local coach companies and were changed every 6 or 7 miles; this was workable over a 13-mile line but began to seem uninviting to a railroad determined to stretch as far as the Ohio.

Consequently, the B & O held a locomotive competition in 1831. Phineas Davis, whose 3½-ton *York* managed to pull 50 tons at 30mph, sold his engine to the Railroad and was appointed chief locomotive engineer. By 1835 horse traction had disappeared, being replaced by just 7 locomotives.

Unlike the L & M, which suffered many casualties in its first years, there were no deaths on the early B & O passenger trains. Even when the first fatality occurred in 1833, it was to a man who had fallen asleep on the track because, it was said, he had been drinking excessively. By 1834 the Railroad had reached Harpers Ferry, and in the following year opened its Washington branch, graced by the granite Thomas Viaduct. It had not yet reached the Ohio, but was regarded as the most experienced line in America, and an example to be followed by the several newer railroads that were being sponsored up and down the seaboard.

Private Enterprise Takes Charge

Although the Baltimore and Ohio Railroad was the first United States public railroad offering a regular service, it was not the first to provide a regular steam train. That distinction was won by the South Carolina Canal and Railroad Company, which used steam right from the start of operations on Christmas Day 1830. The South Carolina, for a while, was the world's longest railway after it reached the Savannah River near Augusta in Georgia. It was then 136 miles long, more than any of the British railways.

The South Carolina Railroad started from Savannah and its initial aim was to secure cotton traffic for the port. In this it succeeded. It also ran a passenger service which covered the first 90 miles from the coast in 10½ hours; passengers then spent the night in rudimentary accommodation before continuing their trip the next morning. Night operations soon became feasible, however, through the introduction of locomotive headlamps; the first experiment was simply a flatcar, supporting a shaded bonfire, pushed ahead of the locomotive, but soon a true locomotive headlamp was developed.

In England, trunk lines were beginning to take shape. The success of the L & M encouraged a new company, the Grand Junction Railway (GJ) to extend the track down to the industrial Midlands. The GJ connected at Birmingham with the London and Birmingham Railway, which had been laboriously laid northward from London by Robert Stephenson. Like others, the Stephensons could turn readily from mechanical to civil engineering although, as time went on, it was found better to employ specialized civil engineers. Already, in the L & M surveys, George Stephenson had displayed incompetence that would not have been tolerated by the directors of later railways.

By 1838 it was possible to travel by train from London to Liverpool and Manchester. Elsewhere, the civic luminaries of ports like Bristol and Southampton had also sponsored railways. The London and Southampton, later the London and South Western (L & SW), linked Southampton to the capital in 1840, while the Great Western Railway reached Bristol in 1841. Of the several other lines, the short London and Greenwich was distinctive in that it was built on a brick viaduct, and the Newcastle and Carlisle was the first coast-to-coast line.

In America, although railroads had enthusiastic sponsors, capital was less readily available than in Britain, so after the B & O's first line was built, there was a tendency to construct low-cost lines. On the other hand, the British lines were solid and carefully engineered, and so lavishly built that for the most part their infrastructure still remains in use, carrying the heavier and faster trains of today. On both sides of the Atlantic there were periods of great optimism, when investors avidly sought railway shares; in Britain there was a 'Railway Mania' when, for a time, any railway share found a ready buyer. This was followed by a crash in 1847 that ruined many families. In the United States, the crash of 1857 included among its victims many small Mid-Western farmers, who had mortgaged their farms to buy shares in the Milwaukee and Mississippi Railroad. This was one of several occurrences that over the years turned initial Mid-Western enthusiasm for railroad companies into deep-seated suspicion.

The first steam locomotive appeared in Chicago as early as 1848, when the *Pioneer* first performed on the new track of the short Galena and Chicago Union Railroad. By 1850 railroads were still rare outside the eastern states, but America could

already claim 9000 miles of railroad. Pennsylvania, New York, and Massachusetts had more than 1000 miles each, and in 1851 the 483-mile New York and Erie Railroad would link the Atlantic with Lake Erie. This was not the first line across New York; after the opening of the Mohawk and Hudson Railroad in 1831, a series of connecting short lines had been created to make a route between Albany and Buffalo which would eventually form the main line of the New York Central System.

It was said that the Mohawk and Hudson's inaugural passenger train covered the 17 miles in 38 minutes. This may have been true as the New York-built *De Witt Clinton*, which hauled it, threw out enough sparks to ruin the clothing of the somewhat exposed passengers. In the following 2 decades American passenger comfort improved. During the 1840s double-truck 8-wheelers began to replace the smaller 4-wheeler passenger

Above: A British cartoon comments on the 1836 railway boom.

Below left: The first Baldwin-built locomotive, ready to haul the first passenger train from Philadelphia in 1832.

Above right: Another early nineteenth-century British cartoon, speculating on what the new technology might bring.

Right: Paddington Station, the London terminus of the Great Western Railway, in the 1860s.

HYDE PARK AS IT WILL BE

cars. These new cars had a central aisle leading to open platforms at each end, but their couplings were still of the loose link-and-pin type. This looseness helped small locomotives to start heavy trains by, as it were, adding the weight of each car successively as the train moved from rest. But this was at the price of considerable jolting that could prove lethal to train-men and passengers moving between the end platforms. Gradually, stoves and washrooms became common on this new breed of 8-wheelers, and some railroads, especially in the south, began to provide cars for ladies that were secure from the over-friendly, over-noisy, tobacco-spitting males who could so readily become unwanted traveling companions.

The typical American passenger train averaged about 15mph in the early 1840s. For most, this seemed commendably fast.

Accidents were frequent, but relatively harmless because of the low speeds. In both Britain and the United States, people often complained about the increasing speeds on precisely this ground. But as signaling and train control improved this argument lost its force until, after mid-century, high speed became a selling point.

In Britain with its more expensive track, speeds reached by the new passenger trains were even higher. By the mid-1840s 60mph was quite frequently attained for short distances, while train schedules demanded average running speeds of about 30mph for first-class trains. Despite these high speeds, there were very few fatalities. In 1842 there were about 24 million passengers in the United Kingdom but only 5 were killed 'from causes beyond their own control.'

Above: Pangbourne Station in the early years of the Great Western Railway. The broad gauge, laid on balks rather than the conventional crossties, is clearly visible.

Left: Construction of the London and Birmingham Railway's Kilsby Tunnel in 1837. The picture shows the pumps needed when unsuspected quicksand was encountered.

Above right: Directors of the Union Pacific conferring in their private railroad car. The line was still under construction; the firearms above the doorway are for immediate use, and so are the spittoons.

Right: The first train from Cape Town arrives at Wellington. This was the real beginning of the South African system, although the standard gauge shown here was later narrowed.

The Networks Evolve

British and United States railroads were laid in the absence of any national railway policy, but elsewhere in the world governments, profiting from this experience, exercised greater control to avoid capital being wasted building unnecessary lines. Belgium was remarkable in that its initial rail network, consisting of 1 north-south and 1 east-west trunk route, was owned and planned by the state. In France private companies were encouraged but were subjected to searching government supervision; as befitted a highly centralized state, the main lines converged on Paris. In Germany the various states organized their own railways, and it was King Ludwig of Bavaria who built the first, 5-mile, line in 1835. Friedrich List, after viewing the pioneer United States railroads, managed to persuade the Saxony government to back his proposal for the first intercity line, from Leipzig to Dresden, which was finished in 1839.

In colonial territories the first lines, usually running from ports into the interior, appeared around mid-century, although the very first was built by the Spanish in Cuba as early as 1837. In Australia, the states of Victoria, New South Wales and South Australia had each opened a short line in the 1850s, followed by New Zealand in 1862. In South Africa, although a 2-mile line at Durban was opened in 1862, the first substantial line was that from Cape Town to Wellington in 1863, followed the next year by the Cape Town to Wynberg line. Both these railways had difficulty recruiting construction workers, and both were opposed by local interests led, quite often, by the clergy. Canada saw its first short railway at Montreal in 1836 and, after the 1854 opening of the 9155-foot bridge across the St Lawrence, the Grand Trunk Railway linked Montreal and Toronto with Portland, Maine.

By 1875 some of the western trunk routes still remained to be built in the United States but in Britain the network was more or

less complete, with principal companies well established. In many respects the London and North Western Railway (L & NWR) was the biggest; it combined the earlier Liverpool and Manchester, Grand Junction, and London & Birmingham railways and ran from London to its main junction at Crewe, and from there to Carlisle, Holyhead, Liverpool and Manchester. It liked to style itself the Premier Line and, in co-operation with the Caledonian Railway in Scotland, operated an Anglo-Scottish west-coast service in competition with a route along the east

coast run by a consortium of 3 other railways; the Great Northern
from London to Yorkshire, the North Eastern up to the border,
and the North British Railway onto Edinburgh. Lying between
these 2 routes was the Midland Railway, which did eventually
run its own London to Scotland service by a circuitous route, but
its spine was from Yorkshire, through Birmingham, down to
Bristol. The west of England was served mainly by the Great
Western Railway (GWR), which faced competition from the
London and South Western between London and Devon, and
from the L & NWR between London and Birmingham, but which
had a monopoly from London to Bristol and South Wales. The
competition that the GWR fought on 2 of its main lines resulted in
a very high standard of service and equipment which also benefitted its Bristol and Welsh services. This competitive stimulus
was less rewarding in the southeast of England, where the cut-
throat rivalry of the South Eastern and London, Chatham and
Dover railways resulted in extremely high standards in some
services, but abysmal standards in many others. South of the
capital the London, Brighton and South Coast Railway served
Brighton and helped to increase land values in the outer suburban areas, while in the agricultural expanses of East Anglia the
Great Eastern had a monopoly, though this was not very remun-

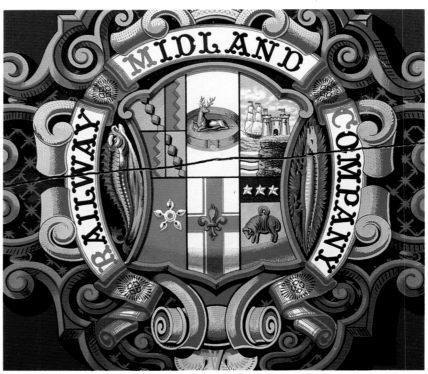

Above left: A stopping train calls at Stratford, Connecticut, in 1867. Arrival of such a train, known as an 'accommodation train' in the United States, was the highpoint of the day for small communities.

Left: The coat of arms of the Midland Railway.

Above right: A Kansas Pacific Railway poster, typical of the publicity material used by Midwestern railroads to entice new settlers.

Right: A modern replica of the celebrated broad-gauge *Iron Duke* locomotive of the Great Western Railway.

Left: A passenger train crossing the first Niagara railway bridge in about 1860. An ordinary boxcar is provided for the mail traffic.

Below: Construction of the Union Pacific Railroad at Green River, Wyoming. The track on the left is temporary, and used for carrying materials.

erative. Other regional monopolies, just managing to pay a dividend most years, could be found in Ireland and also in Scotland, where the Highlands were shared by the Great North of Scotland and the Highland railways.

In this period from 1850 to 1875, railway building continued in the eastern states of America but also spread to the Mid-West and eventually to the Pacific. In the 1850s 4 main routes were laid from the east, across the mountains to Lake Erie or the Ohio. These included the New York and Erie and the newly formed New York Central. The B & O reached the Ohio in 1852, and the Pennsylvania Railroad, following an earlier route which had combined canals, railways, and cable-operated inclines, reached Pittsburgh from Philadelphia in 1852 and then linked up with the associated Pittsburgh, Fort Wayne and Chicago Railroad to provide a through service from Philadelphia to Chicago in 1858.

In the United States the railroad offered a short-cut to the economic development of the wide open spaces in the West that the federal government wished to develop and populate. So from the 1850s subsidies were granted to railroad companies in the form of land grants. Companies were offered federal land along the routes of their projected railroads; these blocks of land, together with the intervening blocks retained by the government, could be expected to rise in value in line with the service provided by the new railroad and so helped to attract investors to the railroad and buyers for the land.

The total length of American railroads had begun to exceed Britain's in the 1830s, and by the mid-1850s the United States owned about 50 percent of the world's mileage. By 1870 United States mileage was 93,000 miles, and still growing. In the prairies, 4 land-grant lines, the Chicago and North Western, the Milwaukee, the Rock Island and the Burlington railroads, were

dominant and, farther west, new lines had been encouraged by the completion of the first transcontinental railroad.

The latter, divided between the Union Pacific Railroad laid westward from Omaha, and the Central Pacific (later Southern Pacific) laid eastward from the Pacific, was the fruit of the Pacific Railway Bill, signed by President Lincoln in 1862. Despite financial mismanagement, and thanks largely to hard work by Chinese and Irish construction gangs, the 2 lines, totaling 1780 miles, linked up in Utah in 1869. The telegraph laid alongside the line conveyed the news that the last, golden, spike had been driven in, and this event of May 10 1869 was recognized then, as later, as a landmark in the United States' progression from a bundle of states to a nation.

The Iron Road

By 1830, the cast-iron rail laid on stone blocks was already obsolete. Instead, wrought-iron rails fixed to crossties (or sleepers) were preferred. These ties provided a cushion for the rails and also prevented them spreading apart. Flat-bottom rail, spiked directly to the ties, was usual in North America and some colonial lines, whereas bullhead rail, seated in cast-iron chairs which themselves were bolted to the crossties, was usual in Britain and parts of Europe. It was only after more than a century that British engineers changed to flat-bottom rail, and in Britain many miles of bullhead track are still in existence.

There were occasional variations, as engineers sought better alternatives. Isambard Kingdom Brunel of the Great Western Railway laid his broad-gauge rails along timber beams, or balks, which themselves were supported by timber piles. He also used bridge rail, whose cross-section was an inverted 'V,' but neither of these innovations survived. President Lord of the Erie Railroad, also a broad-gauge enthusiast, attempted with scant success to lay his track on deep oak piling. Another American innovation was strap rail, in which the rails were made of wood but had a thin strip of iron to provide a running surface. This brought considerable economy of iron, but not of blood, for the iron strip tended to be dislodged by passing trains, to form a 'snakehead' which sometimes burst through the floor.

In North America the underlying philosophy was that railroads should be built cheaply and improved later. For this reason curves were often sharp, with grades tending to follow rather than oppose the lie of the land. Whereas in Britain most railways were double-track, in America the single-track line was standard in the early decades. When serious water obstacles were encountered, it was common for the railroad to terminate at the waterside, and a train ferry provided a connection with the other bank. Accordingly the South Carolina Railroad terminated at Hamburg, opposite Augusta, Georgia, and the Central Pacific ended at Oakland, rather than San Francisco.

Although in the early decades it was clear to many promoters and engineers that sooner or later individual railways would be linked to form complete national networks, this likelihood was not enough to persuade companies to adopt a uniform rail gauge. George Stephenson, by perpetuating the gauge of his colliery line

Above top: Part of the first United States transcontinental ready for its rails. The cheap construction of this line can be seen by the untrimmed green crossties.

Above center: Early track in Pennsylvania, laid on stone blocks.

Left: Cross-sections of early British rail. The Great Western bridge rail (center) was not very successful; nor was the London and Birmingham's reversible rail, designed so that both top and bottom surfaces could then be used.

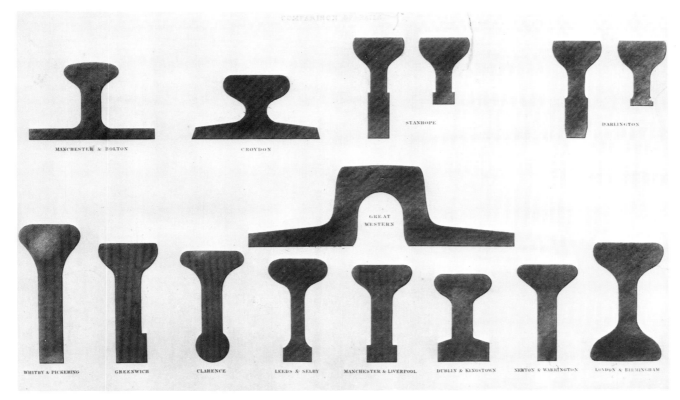

MANCHESTER & BOLTON   CROYDON   STANHOPE   DARLINGTON

GREAT WESTERN

WHITBY & PICKERING   GREENWICH   CLARENCE   LEEDS & SELBY   MANCHESTER & LIVERPOOL   DUBLIN & KINGSTOWN   NEWTON & WARRINGTON   LONDON & BIRMINGHAM

Above: The changing shape and growing size of American rail; the figures show the weight of rail in pounds per yard.

Left: Another view of the Great Western Railway, this time near Reading. The train is broad gauge, but the track is now mixed gauge, a third rail having been laid to accommodate standard-gauge trains.

Below: Strap rail as was used on the B & O Railroad in 1830.

in subsequent railways, founded the standard gauge of 4 feet 8½ inches, and this spread with Stephenson locomotives to the United States and elsewhere. But some American lines chose 4 feet 10 inches, while many railroads of the American South preferred 5 feet. Between New York and Washington, trains of 'compromise cars' were run. These had wide-tread wheels which could run on standard and 4-foot 10-inch gauge tracks.

Most of continental Europe adopted standard gauge, but Portugal, Spain and Russia preferred a wider gauge. Russia's decision to adopt the broad gauge, although attributed by the British press to nefarious strategic aims, was actually taken on the advice of the American Colonel Whistler who had engineered several lines in the southern states of America and naturally recommended the same 5-foot gauge.

In Britain the 7-foot gauge of the Great Western Railway enabled it to provide the fastest and most comfortable trains in the land, but the inability to exchange cars with other railways was a great inconvenience. So the 'narrow-gauge interest' evolved, intent on persuading Parliament to end the GWR gauge, but it was handicapped by the apparent technical superiority of the broad gauge. Eventually the Gauge Act was passed in 1846, specifying that 4 feet 8½ inches was to be the maximum gauge in England, Wales and Scotland (but not in Ireland, where a considerable mileage of 5-foot 3-inch track had been laid).

In the end Britain, with the exception of lines built by the GWR in broad-gauge times, had the most restrictive height and width limitations of all standard-gauge railways. Whereas GWR rolling stock could be almost 11 feet wide and 15 feet high, the present-day standard maximum dimensions for British stock are 9 feet wide and less than 13 feet high. Even the South African Railways, with their 3-foot 6-inch gauge, can use 10-foot-wide vehicles. Continental European dimensions are a few inches greater in width and considerably higher than the British, while United States rolling stock can be somewhat bigger than European, over 16 feet being available vertically and nearly 11 feet horizontally. But the 5-foot gauge Russian railways were, and remain, the best placed, with a height restriction of more than 17 feet and a maximum width of over 11 feet.

Forward from the *Rocket*

Innovation did not end with the *Rocket*. For the Liverpool and Manchester Railway contract, the Stephensons at first built enlarged versions of the *Rocket*, and then the *Northumbrian*, in which for the first time the firebox was not hung onto the back of the boiler, but was part of it. This machine also had a smokebox leading to the chimney, and instead of a water barrel its tender carried an iron tank. Then, still in 1830, came the *Planet*, in which the cylinders were placed beneath the smokebox, between the frames, with their connecting rods driving cranks on the rear axle. From the *Planet* the Stephensons derived the *Patentee*, similar but bigger, with a carrying axle leading and trailing, and a driving axle in the middle (making it a 2-2-2).

Edward Bury, engineer of the London and Birmingham Railway, designed small 4-wheelers (0-4-0) in which bar frames were used, instead of the plate frames preferred by the Stephensons. Bury's locomotives also had the 'haystack' firebox, which was a vertical cylinder terminating in a dome (the predecessor of the steam dome), whose height above the water level enabled fairly dry steam to be drawn off to the cylinders. Bury's locomotives, with their bar frames, were more suited to the rough American track than Stephenson's, and formed the basis for the Norris line of American-built locomotives. Norris retained the bar frames and the haystack firebox, but also provided a leading truck (or bogie) to help the locomotive negotiate sharp curves. The result was an effective outside-cylinder 4-2-0 which sold well not only in the United States, but also abroad; even the British Birmingham and Gloucester Railway bought a batch. During the 1840s this 4-2-0 acquired a leading 4-wheel truck, thereby becoming a 4-4-0. It was the 4-4-0 which from then on was the dominant wheel arrangement on North American railroads until, toward the end of the century, it was superseded by larger types.

Right: Great Western locomotive development during its first 2 decades. *North Star* (top left) was one of the first batch of engines while *Lalla Rookh* (bottom right) dates from the mid-1850s. Much better than the latter was *Iron Duke* (bottom center), representative of a class which lasted up to the end of the broad gauge in the 1890s.

Below: An early locomotive conversion. *Vulcan* was built for the GWR in 1838 and was a passenger locomotive with 8-foot driving wheels. Later the rear frame was extended to carry fuel and water, and the engine thereby became a tank locomotive, as shown here.

Below right: A textbook diagram of an 1848 locomotive.

EARLY LOCOMOTIVE ENGINES OF THE
GREAT WESTERN RAILWAY COMPANY 1837 TO 1855

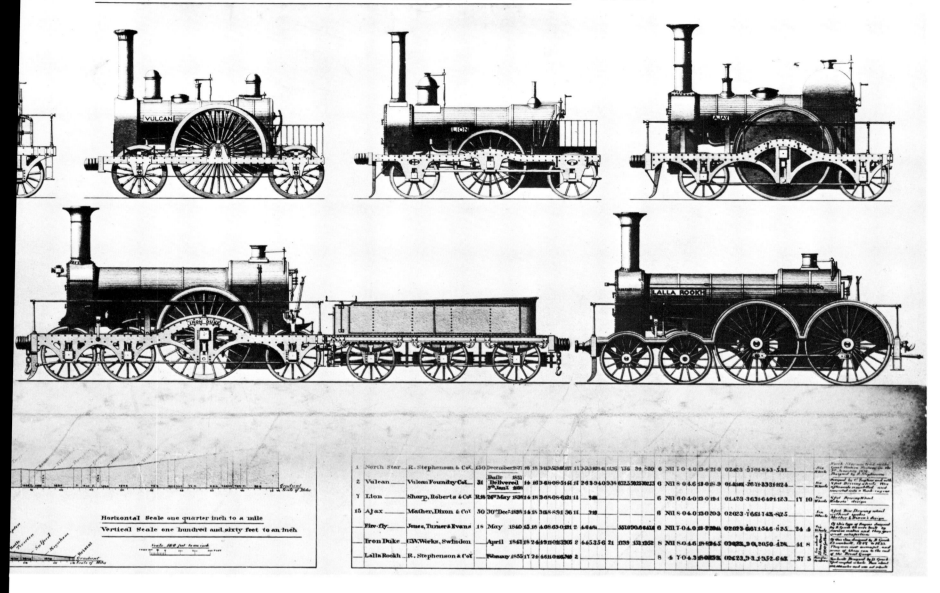

Horizontal Scale one quarter inch to a mile
Vertical Scale one hundred and sixty feet to an inch

LOCOMOTIVE ENGINE

Left: A Baldwin freight locomotive of the 1840s. The tapered boiler, favored in the United States long before it appeared in Britain, can be clearly seen.

Below: A 4-horsepower locomotive, actually built and unsuccessfully tried out in Italy in 1850, the aim being to dispense with the more costly steam locomotive.

Right: A poster of the 1850s, published by the Lake Shore Railroad, which later became part of the New York Central Railroad.

Below right: A train of the New York and Harlem Railroad crossing a trestle close to 4th Avenue in New York.

The leading 4-wheel truck had been devised by John Jervis of the Mohawk and Hudson Railroad, who realized that British-style locomotives were not designed for the sharp curves of American track and with his *Experiment* he showed that a leading, swiveling, truck could solve this problem. Another American innovator was Joseph Harrison, who made the 4-4-0 a viable proposition at the higher speeds with his equalizer, which enabled all 4 driving wheels to absorb bumps in the track. His 4-4-0 *Gowan and Marx* of 1840 weighed 11 tons and pulled a 432-ton Philadelphia and Reading Railroad freight train at an average speed of 10mph.

For the B & O Railroad Ross Winans built his 0-8-0 'Mud-diggers' from 1844. With their 8 coupled wheels, these could start heavy loads without wheel-slip, and were soon followed by the 'Camels,' in which he placed the driver's cab above the boiler. These had plate frames, and burned coal instead of coke.

The last major contribution by Robert Stephenson was the 'long-boiler' configuration in which, by accepting overhang fore and aft, long boiler tubes could be accommodated, thereby extracting more heat from the hot fire gases on their way to the chimney. Meanwhile, Thomas Crampton, in order to accommodate the big driving wheels that were required for high speeds, placed them behind the firebox and so created a very distinctive type which became popular in Germany and France, but was only tried in small numbers in Britain and the United States.

On the broad-gauge Great Western Railway, Daniel Gooch introduced the 'Iron Duke' series in the 1840s. These were large engines with a high boiler pressure of 100 pounds per square inch (psi) and they remained in service for decades. One of these 4-2-2 engines took a 100-ton train 53 miles along the GWR's superb track in just 47 minutes. This was a record no other railway of the world could equal in 1848.

The Early Trains

On Western European railways the highway coach tradition lasted longer than in America, and the rigid-wheelbase 4- or 6-wheel car became the standard rail passenger vehicle for decades. Originally this was virtually 3 or more coach bodies joined together and placed on railway wheels; the compartment style of accommodation, with facing seats, was a coaching configuration that would last to the present day on many railways of the world.

With their 8-wheel, center-aisle, washroom-equipped coaches, the American railroads were well ahead of Europe at an early stage, and eventually several American ideas were adopted in Europe. In Britain the 4- and 6-wheeler survived another 100 years but washrooms were soon necessary as long non-stop runs became more common. There were several ingenious attempts to introduce these without providing central aisles or side corridors, but eventually the British long-distance train was provided with corridors. Corridors implied non-revenue space, and so to compensate for this both trains and passenger cars tended to become longer, and the long, fast-running, passenger car required an American-style chassis on swiveling trucks (called bogies in Britain).

The long distances run by American trains led to the development of sleeping cars. This was not purely an American idea, for the London and Birmingham Railway had provided rudimentary convertible bed carriages in the early 1840s. In the 1850s several American inventors sold their sleeping car ideas to individual

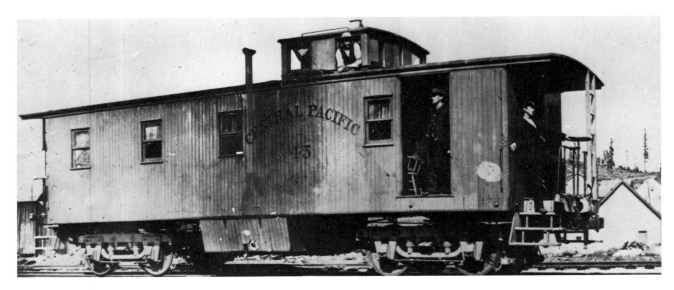

Left: A caboose of the Central Pacific Railroad, photographed in about 1885.

Below: Early oil transport in the United States. This picture was made in about 1868 near Rouseville, Pennsylvania.

Right: One of the earlier Pullman sleeping cars, built in 1869.

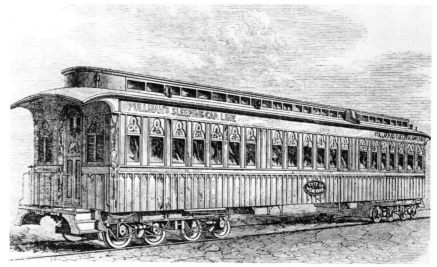

railroads, which faced the problem that sleeping cars accommodated far fewer revenue passengers. Various methods of converting seats into narrow berths were patented to overcome this difficulty, and in the 1850s George Pullman produced a car incorporating several of these ideas. Pullman was not particularly inventive, but he had marketing skills and was attracted by the idea of the 'hotel on wheels.' His company slowly overcame its competitors and operated Pullman cars on an increasing number of United States long-distance services.

Pullman also operated parlor cars and dining cars, and soon

the basic class distinction on United States railroads was between those who paid extra to travel Pullman, and those who did not, traveling 'coach.' In Britain and Europe class distinctions were more refined. From 1844 British lines were required to run at least one daily train for third-class passengers at a low fare and reasonable speed. Many railways responded by providing the most spartan accommodation possible, but as the years passed, the number of third-class passengers increased and they became highly profitable, so some small improvements were made. Nevertheless, for those unable to endure third-class travel, and unable to afford first, second-class accommodation was then provided.

The rigidity of the British class distinctions was eroded when the Midland Railway, in a bid to attract first-class passengers from rival lines, imported American Pullman cars in 1874. It became evident that even on British track the United States-style suspension provided a more comfortable ride, and so the Midland began to build bogie vehicles (with 4-wheel trucks) for its other services. Having taken one step, it was easy to take another; third-class passengers were allowed to travel on all trains. This change was achieved by withdrawing third-class vehicles, eliminating second class, and reclassifying second-class cars as thirds. With these improvements the Midland duly attracted passengers from rival lines and the other British companies began to follow suit.

The Pullman concept, however, did not thrive in Britain, where journeys were short and first-class travel provided all the amenities required by the wealthy. But in continental Europe the Belgian Nagelmackers introduced a service very similar to that of George Pullman. Nagelmackers' cars were a little more luxurious than Pullman's, and were intended to run in international services. He had to face competition from the American William Mann, but in 1876 the 2 rivals merged to form the International Sleeping Car Company, or Wagons-Lits.

In the early 1870s the fastest New York to Chicago train averaged 30mph. In Britain speeds were also creeping upward. Long station meal breaks were being eliminated, and running speeds often exceeded 50mph. The *Flying Scotsman* was scheduled to run the 392 miles from London to Edinburgh in 9½ hours, and it averaged 48mph for the first 76 miles.

Although it was passenger services that aroused greatest public interest and which made or unmade a railway's reputation, the majority of the world's railways obtained most of their revenue from freight operations. In the late 1840s the London and North Western Railway was despatching daily from London 6 night and 4 day freight trains. These consisted, typically, of some 40 tarpaulin-shrouded cars, most of which weighed 3 tons when empty and 6 tons loaded.

At that period, both in Britain and America, consignments were usually quite small, and consisted of high-value goods that could easily bear the cost of transportation. But by the 1870s bulk freight was beginning to predominate. Coal was the most import-

FIRST CLASS.

SECOND CLASS.

Good night Ma

Sleeping Car — going to Bed.

a Smoke

Private-Room

Dawn — Is it time to get up?

Very refreshing

Confound it! How the fellow snores.

Quiet Luncheon

THE RAILWAY QUESTION — NOTES IN A PULLMAN PALACE CAR ON THE MIDLAND RAILWAY

Above left: Going to the races by first-class train in Britain, in the early 1840s.

Above center: British second-class passengers board their train for the races.

Above right: The third-class passengers make the best of things on their way to the races.

Left: A British magazine views the novel experience of traveling by Pullman sleeper on the Midland Railway.

Right center: The New York Central's 'Fast Mail' arrives at Chicago for the first time. The last 4 vehicles were operated by the United States Post Office.

Below right: The freight shed at Bristol, one of the largest of such buildings in Britain.

Overleaf: The South Eastern Railway's terminus at Charing Cross, built in 1864 to bring the company's trains right into the heart of London. The roof collapsed in 1905, with considerable loss of life.

THIRD CLASS.

ENGLAND IN 1842: GOING TO THE DERBY.

DRAWN BY JOHN LEECH.

ant in this category, and companies like the rich North Eastern Railway and the small Taff Vale in Wales made their living by hauling coal in block trains at low rates but correspondingly low costs. These 2 railways, like others, were also in the docks business, building their own wharves so as to provide an integrated export service. By the early 1880s the Cardiff docks, essentially a railway creation, were exporting 8 million tons of Welsh coal annually. There was a similar situation in the United States,

where railroads in Pennsylvania were already handling heavy coal tonnages in the 1860s, while those in the Mid-West were beginning to handle grain. In the 1860s the 'fast freight lines' were set up by freight agencies, which would load their own cars and despatch them over routes consisting of several adjacent railroads. This eliminated the costly transhipments suffered by most freight, because the railroads were still not passing railroad-owned cars through from one company to another.

In the 1840s 8-wheel freight cars were in common use in the United States. As early as the 1850s the Baltimore and Ohio Railroad was using all-metal 20-ton coal hoppers, although this was not typical of American railroads at that time. Wooden boxcars were predominant, although flatcars and gondolas were also popular. Stock cars for moving cattle were the most common type of specialized vehicle, but the first successful refrigerator car would appear in 1877.

Crew cars, or cabooses, required by the numerous train staff (conductor, trainman, and brake-men) were attached to the tail of United States freight trains from the early years, and in the 1860s they began to be fitted with observation cupolas, from which the train could be watched; hot axle boxes, unless spotted early, could set trains on fire. With heavy trains and steep grades, braking American freight trains demanded a complement of brake-men who, responding to locomotive whistle signals, would mount the roofs of the cars to tighten the brake wheels. In Britain, freight trains were stopped at the tops of inclines so that a proportion of the car brakes could be pinned down. At other times, on level track, the guard, traveling in his heavily ballasted brakevan at the rear, could screw down its brakes and this, together with the locomotive brakes, would slow the train.

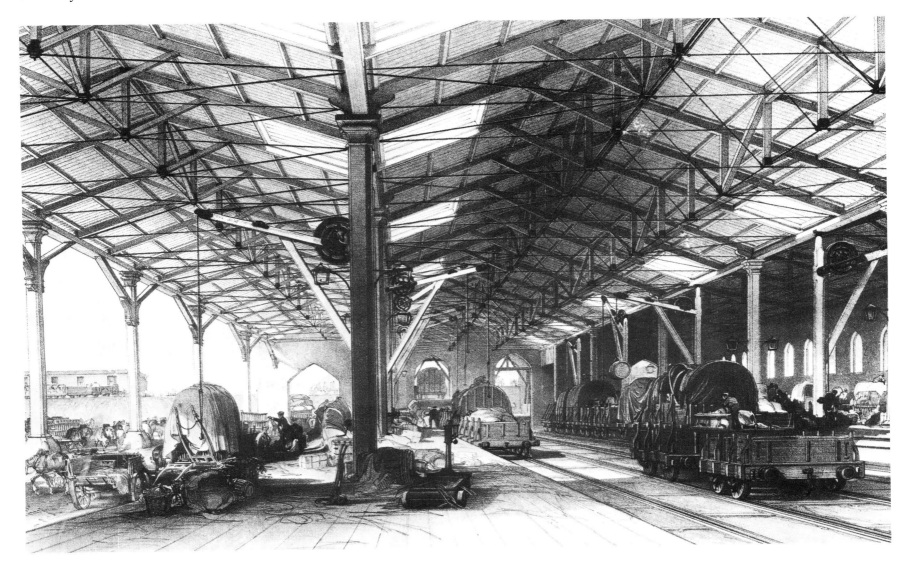

The Railroad at War

As early as the 1830s the British army had used the Liverpool and Manchester Railway to speed the despatch of troops to Ireland, but in the American Civil War the whole campaign was dominated by the ease with which the opposing sides could shift masses of troops and supplies.

The South, which had most need of good transportation, was handicapped because, having taken up arms on the principle that outside interference was intolerable, it was reluctant to impose much-needed central control over the 113 different railroad companies in its territory. Thus companies that had long resisted the linking of their lines with adjacent railroads continued to do so, and when soldiers laid lines along city streets to effect just such connections, they were abused by the companies and the local populace.

In the absence of central control, it was the Confederate army officers who began to direct railroad operations. This added yet another obstacle to the efficient functioning of the southern network, as the officers, overriding the advice of railroad managers, hindered operations by hoarding empty freight cars for their own possible use, sending off trains in one direction without making provision for the return of locomotives and stock, and threatening any of the railroaders who dared to dissent with courts-martial.

The Federal government did much better than the Confederates, setting a pattern for other governments in future wars. It did not impose army officers as managers. Instead, it gave railroad managers military rank, so that they could not be intimidated by regular officers and were more or less free to balance war needs against railroad necessities. The United States Military Railroads Administration was also formed to operate those lines built or, as was the vital Philadelphia, Wilmington and Baltimore, directly taken over, by the government.

For the South, the cheap structural standards of the United-

States railroads proved to be especially damaging. With practically no heavy industry in its territory, it was unable to replace worn-out rails and rolling stock. One northern general, viewing a train proceeding along recently captured southern track, compared the scene to a fly crawling over a corrugated washboard. Both sides soon made raids to wreck their enemy's railroads, and it was the South which had most difficulty in repairing the acute damage caused.

The tactical importance of the railroads was recognized early, for the very first major battle, Bull Run, was won by the South after it had successfully brought up reinforcements by trains which ejected their complements virtually on the battlefield. The South, too, was initially most successful in raiding enemy railroads. Stonewall Jackson once managed to surround 56 of the B & O's locomotives. He carried off about 12 of these as trophies, hauled over the highway by horse teams, and wrecked the rest, thereby closing down the B & O main line for several months.

As the war progressed, the northerners became more skilled in

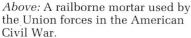

Above: A railborne mortar used by the Union forces in the American Civil War.

Left: Union troops at Alexandria waiting to go into action by train. The locomotive belongs to the small, but key, Orange and Alexandria Railroad, and has been taken over by the military.

Above right: One of the most common methods for damaging track; when the wood was ignited the half-melted rails would bend out of shape, by their own weight.

Right: A locomotive comes to grief on the long-suffering Orange and Alexandria Railroad.

railroad destruction. Their Andrews Raid, which became famous as the Great Locomotive Chase, was foiled through the tenacity of a southern railroader, the resulting chase ending when the locomotive commandeered by the raiders ran out of fuel. At first, to destroy railroads, raiders simply removed and bent the rails round nearby trees, but it was easy to correct that kind of damage. A northern officer was soon telling his men that rails should be rolled up like doughnuts, and by the time Sherman began his march through Georgia, he had been equipped with a machine that heated rails and then twisted them like corkscrews.

Another Federal innovation was the Railroad Construction Corps, an army organization which had the responsibility to construct and maintain military railroads. This idea was noticed in Prussia, which in imitation introduced railroad operating regiments. When the Franco-Prussian War broke out in 1870 the German railways were well prepared and had some success in the first few weeks. However, later, when the battles moved onto

French territory, supplies were slow in coming up, with transit times so long that meat was often foul-smelling by the time it was delivered. German locomotives and rolling stock were used inside occupied France, but as French bridges were lower than German, a number of locomotive chimneys were knocked off; from then on Prussian locomotives were designed with 2-piece chimneys, the cap being detachable.

Where the German railways excelled was in the mobilization period, troop movements and schedules having been planned meticulously in advance. The Prussian conscription system, which entailed army service for all young men and the creation of a 'citizens' army' of ex-conscript reservists, depended on the railways to carry reservists to their army depots and then, with their regiments, to the front. Other continental European governments soon followed the Prussian example, thereby taking a long step toward total war, a concept that would not have been possible before the Railway Age.

A. Gelly, Char... (...production interdite). - Imp. Van Praet

4. Mézières. — Destruction du pont du Chemin de fer en 1871, avant le passage d'un train

Above: A German military train fallen from a sabotaged bridge in France during the Franco-Prussian War. French partisans and saboteurs were so active that the Prussians began to place a local hostage on each locomotive.

Left: A United States Military Railroad train passes a guarded bridge on the Orange and Alexandria Railroad.

Right: Years later, survivors of the 'Great Locomotive Chase' pose in front of a memorial to that event in Chattanooga.

Locomotive Development 1850-1875

Locomotives developed steadily during the 25 years between 1850 and 1875. Change was directed more to improvement and enlargement than to radical redesign. New wheel arrangements were introduced to permit bigger locomotives, cabs began to be provided on most engines, and better manufacture, including a growing use of steel, made locomotives safer and more reliable.

John Ramsbottom in Britain and William Mason in the United States are good examples of engineers who improved on tradition and produced superb locomotives. The Mason 4-4-0 gave classic form to that wheel arrangement and, both aesthetically and technically, surpassed its predecessors. Mason used components that were carefully machined so that they would fit snugly, without caulking, his holes were bored so that bolts would fit tightly, and he avoided open seams. By placing his cylinders horizontally, alongside a 4-wheel leading truck of extended wheelbase, he enhanced both appearance and stability.

The so-called 'Mason bogies' were less handsome. Mason initially built these for narrow-gauge lines, considering that the 4-4-0, with its firebox constrained by the driving wheels flanking it, was unsuitable for such lines. They were an Americanized version of the locomotive patented by the Scotsman, Robert Fairlie, in 1864. Fairlie was also trying to solve the problem of providing powerful motive power for sharply curved narrow-gauge lines. The Fairlie locomotive was articulated (jointed) and had 2 pivoting bogie-and-cylinder units, each carrying a boiler, placed back-to-back with the cab in the middle. His *Little Wonder*, working on the narrow-gauge and mountainous Ffestiniog Railway in Wales from 1870, attracted visitors from all over the world and many of them placed orders for the type. Mason's variant, beginning with his *Onward* of 1872, had a single boiler supported by a truck, which accommodated the 4 driving wheels and the cylinders, with the rear section, bolted to the firebox, consisting of the tender mounted on another 4-wheel truck. Despite the steam leaks inevitable with jointed steampipes, these locomotives were successful, and about 150 were built. These were not all of identical design, although Mason was one of the first American locomotive engineers to standardize components.

Locomotive standardization was more advanced in Britain, and Ramsbottom's 'DX' 0-6-0 freight locomotive, a very simple and reliable design, was built for the London and North Western Railway in unprecedented numbers, totaling no fewer than 943

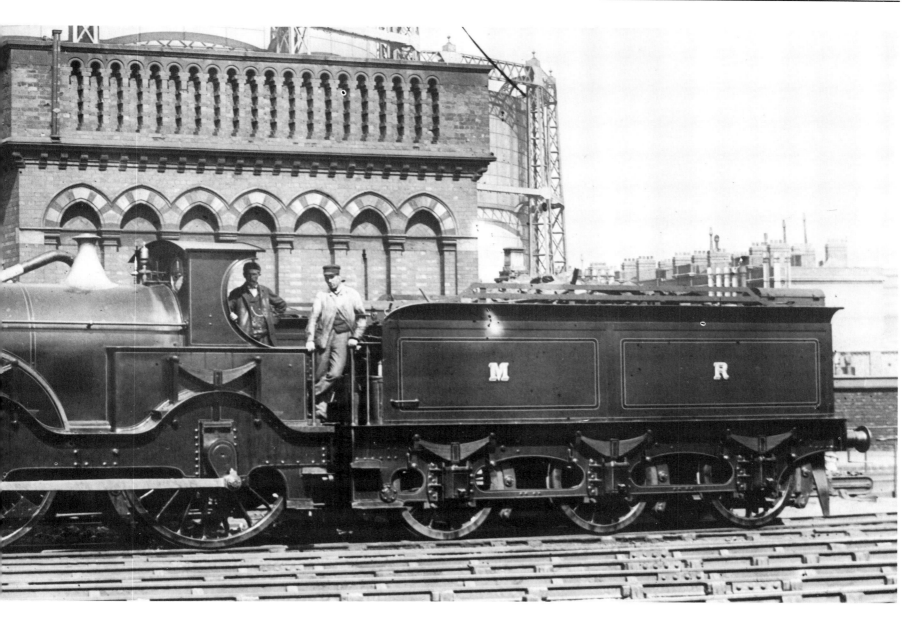

Above: One of Kirtley's 2-4-0 fast passenger locomotives. As with most British locomotives of the period, inside cylinders were used, and also double frames, which could hold a loose driving wheel in place, should the driving axle break.

Left: A 2-6-0, or 'Mogul,' of the Denver and Rio Grande Railroad built in 1871. This wheel arrangement was beginning to be favored in the United States for freight work.

Below left: a fast 2-4-0 of the Paris-Orléans Railway. By this period French locomotives had acquired a distinctive style, very different from that of the British 2-4-0, shown in the above right photograph.

Right: A London and North Western Railway passenger locomotive, built at the Railway's Crewe works in 1862 and rebuilt before this 1907 picture was taken.

units when production ceased. Ramsbottom was the inventor of track troughs for watering locomotives at speed; these were widely used in Britain, and also by the Pennsylvania Railroad. He also designed a speedometer, and a sight-feed lubricator, which enabled engine-men to check oil levels at a glance. His safety valve, based on 2 vertical tubes, hummed loudly just as blowing-off pressure was reached.

Coke, or wood, had been the usual locomotive fuel in the first decades, but in the 1850s ways were found to burn coal efficiently. In America, the locomotive builder Matthias Baldwin experimented with a deflector plate inside the firebox; this tended to burn up, but a firebrick structure proved suitable and was used on the Pennsylvania Railroad in 1854. The aim was to lengthen the path of the hot gases passing through the firebox so as to provide a greater opportunity for coal particles to be burned up, rather than wasted through the chimney. The final solution came from Matthew Kirtley of Britain's Midland Railway, and was a brick arch which forced the gases to pass back over the fire before entering the boiler tubes.

In order to burn small coal, which was plentiful in his home country, Belgium, Alfred Belpaire replaced the high, narrow, firebox with one of his own design. When fully developed, the Belpaire boiler had a square firebox, which provided an increased grate area. It was more costly to build than a round-top firebox, but produced better results. Throughout the rest of the steam era some engineers preferred the round-top, and some the Belpaire.

Kirtley's progression from the 'Single' (engines with a single pair of large-diameter driving wheels) to the 2-4-0 for passenger work typified many British engineers' work of this period. At first they continued to use double frames, with the driving wheels sandwiched between them to avoid disaster, should a driving axle fracture. Eventually, however, axle manufacturing techniques improved so much that single frames could be used, so saving considerable weight and expense.

By this time, the American and British styles of locomotive were very different, although good ideas crossed the Atlantic in both directions. British railway companies tended to establish their own locomotive design and construction facilities, where locomotives that were both obviously British and yet characteristic of a particular railway, were produced. British locomotive-building companies had to rely increasingly on exports. In the United States there were also railroads, for example the Pennsylvania Railroad, which built their own locomotives, but locomotive companies provided the bulk of requirements. Some of these companies, like Baldwin in Philadelphia and the American Locomotive Company (Alco) which developed at Schenectady from the Brooks and other works, were destined to grow into huge corporations which would survive well into the next century.

Above: Another design of inside-cylinder British-built 6-wheeler. This class of locomotive was built in Manchester for the New South Wales Railways from 1877 and was still in use when this photograph was taken, 95 years later.

Right: A 'Single' of the Great Northern Railway, a type that hauled the *Flying Scotsman* in the 1870s. This is No 1, which has been preserved in working order.

PART 2

THE GOLDEN AGE: 1876-1914

Worldwide Expansion

Well before 1875 railways had shown that they were destined to be the principal feature of the nineteenth century's economic landscape, and it was not long before it became evident that their dominance would also be social and military; there was hardly an aspect of human existence that in one way or another had been unaffected by the coming of the railway.

In the small, densely peopled countries of Europe, including Britain, the population had almost daily contact with the railways. They made it possible to live a healthy distance from the place of work, they enabled production of commodities to be concentrated in those areas where conditions were most suitable for production, rather than be scattered in areas close to the consumers. They enabled families to go away for their annual holidays, and for new towns to be used as leisure resorts. They also enabled the newspapers of the capital to be read the same day in the most distant corners of the country. In the United States, the same picture could be seen in the regions of the larger cities, but elsewhere the railroad, while bringing communities closer, did not bring them into the same kind of new intimacy as in Europe; the distances and the differences were too great. In the newer colonial countries, there were areas, such as the hinterlands of Melbourne, Sydney, Cape Town and Toronto, where the railway seemed to be everywhere and all-powerful; however, there were also vast areas not far away where the railway had not penetrated, and indeed would never penetrate. Meanwhile, along the few long-distance routes, communities would develop around the railway stations; some of them were destined to blossom and become townships, while others would remain undistinguished.

In America the feeling of national unity, which flared briefly when the Union Pacific and Central Pacific linked up as the first transcontinental railroad, was short-lived. But in other countries, and internationally, the moral and binding force of a railway route would be acknowledged openly when other transcontinentals, like the Canadian Pacific, Trans-Australian, and Trans-Siberian railways were undertaken. Moreover, it was not always a question of binding nations, but sometimes of binding empires. The Cape to Cairo Railway, never completed, was to cement British control from the top to the bottom of Africa. The mixed rail and ship service, from London through France and Italy to Egypt and from there to India and the East, was in a real sense the main nerve of the British Empire east of Suez.

In Britain, although railways were owned by shareholders and run by managers whose first duty was to provide a dividend, people did believe that the companies were sympathetic to the national (or local) interest. In the United States, for good reason, the average citizen felt that the railroad companies were only interested in making a profit. What was worse was that they were controlled by men intent on a quick profit and fast getaway; men ready to milk the area the company served by extracting high charges from their clients and by running down the capital value of the lines they controlled and on which the whole community ultimately depended.

The Granger movement, which united farmers of the Mid-West and gained great political momentum, was fired by resentment felt by farmers against railroad freight rates. They alleged these were so monstrously high as to keep their produce out of the eastern markets unless they sold it at a ridiculously cheap price to the wholesalers.

By the end of the century, this movement, and other organizations were succeeding in obtaining federal controls over the railroads, limiting their freedom to fix freight rates, to offer rebates to favored clients, and to make inter-railroad rates agreements. In Britain in the same period, there was similarly a tightening of central control, but for different reasons. In the 1840s and 1850s, just when the British railways were in their most formative period, the party system in Parliament was weak. This meant that just a few members representing the railway interest could cripple legislative attempts to impose greater control over the companies. With the consolidation of the party system in the 1860s, the railway companies lost this advantage and over the next decades the government's Board of Trade was able to exercise greater control. This control resulted in better railway safety when, for example, the railways were compelled to instal automatic brakes or block signaling, and to limit railwaymen's working hours. However, attempts to regulate freight rates were less successful and culminated in a situation where the railways found it difficult either to raise or lower their rates.

Growing interest and understanding of railway transport shown in Congress and Parliament was echoed in the public at large, which began to concern itself not only in how railway policy might affect its own particular interests, but also in the details of railway operation and engineering. This was a period when the railways were seeking to impress the populace with big

Previous spread: A construction train of the Northern Pacific Railroad in 1886. This was a transcontinental line which started from Duluth in Minnesota and reached the Pacific at Tacoma in 1887.

Left: As the nineteenth century progressed, once-inaccessible American territories were penetrated by the railroad. This picture shows a train in the mineral-rich Sierra Nevada.

Above: The new station at Darlington, soon after opening in 1887. This was one of many British stations using light steel arches to support a glass roof. The Stockton and Darlington Railway's first locomotive, then preserved at this station, can be glimpsed between 2 of the columns.

Right: A Western Australian Government Railways Perth to Kalgoorlie train makes a stop on its journey. This photograph was taken in about 1900.

schemes like the Forth Bridge and Severn Tunnel in Britain, the new terminals in Manhattan, and the well-publicized operation of fast trains. There was now a section of the public wanting even more detailed knowledge, and railway publications appeared, which provided comprehensive information but were intended neither for railway employees not for investors. What was later known as the Golden Age of railways also witnessed the emergence of the railway enthusiast.

In the United States, total railroad mileage reached an all-time peak in 1916, at 254,000 miles. Much of the mileage built over the previous decades had not been really needed, and was destined for a short life. Traffic had been increasing, but profits had not, and a sixth of the mileage was already in the hands of receivers and trustees. In that year there was an intervention by the federal government that forced the railroads to grant a reduced working day (in effect, and intention, an increase of the average railroader's pay). Other costs, like coal, had also gone up, but railroads were not allowed to adjust their rates to cover these. In 1916 almost 500,000 motor trucks were already registered in the United States, and the first regular air service (New York to Washington) was only 2 years away. Clearly, the railroads faced a tough future.

The situation facing Britain's railways was similar. For them, the last year of the so-called Golden Age was 1914, not 1916, but they also had been deprived of the freedom to set rates at a time when their costs were rising. They did not yet face highway competition, still less airway competition, but the alternative competing technology was visible. They, also, faced a tough future, aggravated by the 4 years of hard use and deferred maintenance that World War I would bring.

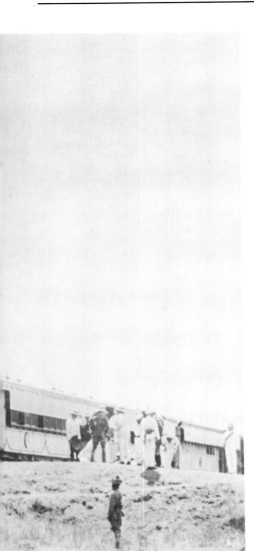

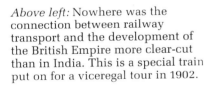

Above left: Nowhere was the connection between railway transport and the development of the British Empire more clear-cut than in India. This is a special train put on for a viceregal tour in 1902.

Left: A passenger train in India.

Above right: A highly decorated royal train provided by the London Brighton and South Coast Railway. Even the coal has been whitewashed.

Right: The Baghdad Railway, financed and built by Germans, is a good example of the geopolitical railway. The project alarmed London by its threat of bringing German influence into the Middle East, but it was not finished until after Germany's defeat in 1918.

Overleaf: The Nordbahn Station in Vienna in 1875. Holding the multinational Austro-Hungarian Empire together was a prime objective of the Austrian railway system.

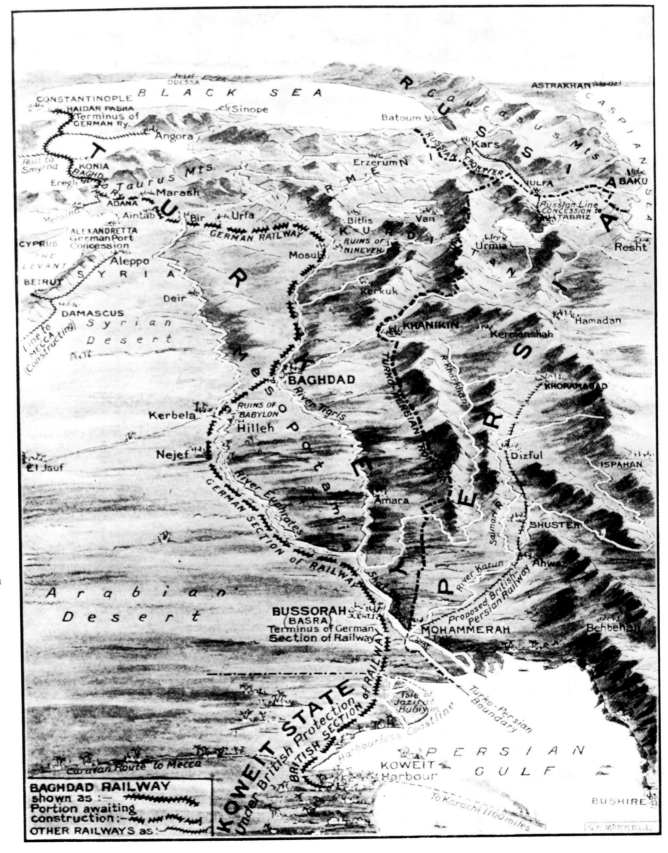

The Gauge Connection

When the first railways were built they were short and isolated, and although a few engineers visualized a time when they would link up to form nationwide networks, there was no pressing need for companies to agree on a standard width between the rails so that rolling stock could run from one railway to another. Moreover there were some managers who found the idea of through running very distasteful, arousing nightmare visions of a railway finding itself denuded of rolling stock in a peak traffic period because adjoining railways were receiving, but not returning, its freight cars. Also, towns at the break of gauge points between railways did well out of the situation, because the transhipment of freight and its cartage through the streets to another terminal represented valuable employment and income.

Added to all this was technical uncertainty over the best gauge for a railway. It was generally thought that a narrow gauge was cheaper to build, especially in hilly areas where its short radius curves cheapened construction markedly, whereas the broader gauges accommodated trains of greater capacity traveling safely at higher speeds.

The coexistence in some parts of the United States of 4-foot 8½-inch, 4-foot 10-inch and 5-foot gauges was just as much an obstacle to low-cost long-distance transportation as the coexistence in Britain of the standard 4 feet 8½ inches with the GWR's 7 feet. It is quite likely that, left to themselves, the British and American companies would have never agreed on a standard gauge. This was something that required political intervention. In Britain the intervention came very early, with Parliament establishing a Gauge Commission to decide whether the 4-foot 8½-inch or the 7-foot gauge should be standardized. This Commission held comparative trials in which the Stephenson interest (standard gauge) put up a markedly inferior performance to that of the Great Western Railway (broad gauge). Nevertheless, because there was so much more standard gauge than broad gauge in Britain, the Commissioners decided that the broad gauge should not be extended. For a few more decades the GWR kept its broad-gauge track to the west, and laid mixed-gauge (3-rail) tracks on most of its mileage. Finally, in 1892, over a meticulously planned weekend, the broad gauge was converted to standard gauge.

In the United States a final decision on gauge came later, and standardization resulted not from governmental coercion, but from the federal choice of 4 feet 8½ inches for the first transcontinental railroad. This gave the standard gauge a valuable seal of approval at a time when it was used on barely 50 percent of United States mileage.

Until the American gauge was standardized, various expedients were used to handle long-distance through traffic. Transhipment, although costly and time-consuming, was the most common method of handling long-distance freight. For passengers, a change of train, and usually of station, was the familiar and much-resented procedure. Just as in England, where critics as well as cartoonists liked to exaggerate the hardships of the break of gauge at Gloucester, so in America these enforced tramps along station tracks built up a powerful public opinion in support of gauge standardization.

The Illinois Central and the Erie railroads, which both interchanged traffic with 5-foot gauge lines at Cairo on the Mississippi, had car-lifting equipment, which transferred car bodies from one set of trucks to another. Elsewhere in the United States it became common to lay a third rail so that mixed-gauge trackage was created.

When it was decided to build the transcontinental at 4 feet 8½ inches instead of the original 5 feet (recommended because most

Californian lines were 5 feet), existing Mid-Western companies with non-standard gauges began to conform. In 1880 the main line of the Erie Railroad across New York was converted from 6 feet to standard in the course of a day. Nevertheless, even after this major conversion a fifth of United States mileage was non-standard. Most of this was in the South, where much 5-foot gauge survived. But in 1881 the Illinois Central, which was standard gauge in its northern reaches, converted its southern main line to standard gauge. This was a line of almost 550 miles, and the conversion was achieved on a Friday, using about 3000 carefully instructed workers who were required to move 1 of the 2 rails 3½ inches closer to the other.

Other southern companies then agreed among themselves to

Above: An 1846 cartoon decrying the chaos of transhipment from broad to narrow gauge at Gloucester.

Above center: Another anti-GWR cartoon, illustrating equine objections to break-of-gauge transhipment.

Above right: 20 May 1892 on the GWR in Devon. The last broad-gauge train from London passes over track ready for conversion to standard gauge.

Right: The last through broad-gauge train from London to the West Country, ready to leave Paddington. This is the same train as the one illustrated above, although with a different, faster, engine for the London to Bristol section.

standardize in the spring of 1886. In preparation, just as the British GWR had built locomotives easily convertible from broad to standard gauge, the Baldwin Locomotive Works built a series of convertible engines for these southern lines. The conversion was not to 4 feet 8½ inches, but to 4 feet 9 inches, which was the gauge of the nearby Pennsylvania Railroad. However, over the years this ½-inch difference, which was negligible in practice, disappeared.

Gauge differences were a characteristic of the British Empire, and the consequences are still apparent. Some territories, such as South Africa, had the good fortune to standardize early but in others, notably India and Australia, a multi-gauge network became permanent. What happened in South Africa was that the

Left: Mixed-gauge track at an industrial site in India.

Right: Mixed gauge at Merida in Mexico. A United States-built 3-foot gauge 4-4-0 leaves, on the left, while a standard-gauge 4-6-0, also built in the United States, awaits its next duty.

Below: A South African picture showing the difference between the 2-foot and the 3-foot 6-inch gauges. The latter is the standard gauge in South Africa, but in many countries both would be regarded as narrow gauges.

first railway was built to the 4-foot 8½-inch gauge, probably because the British locomotive builders recommended and preferred to supply engines of that gauge. But when the need came to push the railway from Cape Town northward from Wellington to Worcester, the surveyor said it was only possible to break through the mountain range with a 2-foot 6-inch gauge, because of the need for sharp curves. Once through the mountains, however, it was clear that a narrow gauge would be disadvantageous. In the end, the 3-foot 6-inch gauge was chosen by the Cape parliament as a compromise, and thereby became the South African standard. When the line through the Hex River Pass was completed, the existing Cape Town to Wellington line became mixed gauge for a few years.

Australia was less fortunate. The British government, bearing in mind the trouble experienced with the Great Western broad gauge at home, was anxious that each of the colonies in Australia should have the same gauge. Australia's first railway, from Melbourne to Port Melbourne, was of the 5-foot 3-inch gauge, whereas the second, from Sydney to Parramatta, was 4 feet 8½ inches. The New South Wales administration was persuaded to change to 5 feet 3 inches, but before doing so it reduced the salary of its chief engineer, who resigned. His successor, from England, was a strong supporter of the 4-foot 8½-inch gauge, and persuaded the New South Wales government to continue with that gauge. Any hope of a standard gauge for Australia was thereby lost. Later, Western Australia and Queensland chose 3 feet 6 inches, South

Australia stayed with adjacent Victoria on the 5-foot 3-inch gauge while Tasmania, starting with 5 feet 3 inches for its Launceston to Deloraine line in 1871, soon changed its mind and adopted 3 feet 6 inches. It was not until the 1960s that major constructions alleviated the Australian gauge problem. A standard-gauge line was laid from Albury in New South Wales to Melbourne, another standard-gauge line in Western Australia connected Perth with the 4-foot 8½-inch gauge Trans-Australian Railway, while the latter, at its eastern end, connected with a standard-gauge line from Port Pirie in South Australia to Broken Hill in New South Wales, making it possible to run 4-foot 8½-inch gauge trains from Sydney to Perth. Another state capital, Brisbane, had been connected to the New South Wales gauge by a 95-mile line in 1930.

In India, where a multi-gauge system has become almost an accepted way of life, the 5-foot 6-inch gauge was initially standardized. Later, when the British authorities wished to add secondary routes, they found that the expense of broad-gauge track was an obstacle. So it was decided that the new lines, which had been carefully planned to connect with the broad-gauge trunk routes, would be of meter gauge. This meter-gauge network still coexists with the broad gauge, and there are also several short narrow-gauge lines. The latter were limited to very local services, but a lack of co-operation between British government departments allowed the adoption of 2 different narrow gauges; 2 feet and 2 feet 6 inches.

Unscrupulous Operators

In 1857 the registrar of Britain's Great Northern Railway was found guilty of embezzling a quarter of a million pounds sterling of the company's funds, and was sentenced to be transported to Australia. The railways, big businesses in which large numbers of employees handled money in offices remote from close supervision, presented great opportunities for the dishonest. As time passed, the companies found ways of regulating crime, and the huge burden of paperwork imposed on station workers is one consequence of this drive against dishonesty. Keeping elaborate records was the first step toward rooting out misappropriations.

However, while petty theft was energetically prosecuted, large-scale misuse of public money was sometimes permissible, provided no criminal intent could be proved. The big railway 'kings' or 'barons' were unscrupulous operators who were intent on enriching themselves at the expense, ultimately, of people poorer than themselves. The United States was a far more sympathetic environment for these people than Britain, where sharp practice, once it became evident, was soon dealt with. In the United States there was an element of public opinion that could be relied on to support the successful buccaneer, and indeed the names of the most successful 'robber barons' have entered into American folklore in the guise almost of heroic figures, which they were not.

In Britain, George Hudson was the best-known and biggest of these men. His heyday was in the 1840s, after he had received a legacy enabling him to change from shopkeeper to railway-share speculator. Soon his bullying, wheedling, and unscrupulous relationships with his fellow-men brought him high responsibility and his sharp share dealings gained him control of 20 percent of the railway mileage. He also became a Tory member of Parliament. This gave him an additional advantage since it enabled him to speak his mind about rival railway companies; companies that threatened to build lines into the territory of his own railways, or companies that had railways in territories which he himself intended to invade. Influencing Parliament to refuse railway proposals, and dissuading investors from putting money into them, were his main lines of attack.

By forcing down rival companies' shares, and then buying

them up, Hudson acquired control of a succession of small companies, which he joined to form large railways, notably the North Eastern and the Midland. In doing this he became part of a process of amalgamation that was demanded by the times, and his defenders claimed that although he might be unscrupulous, his activities did at least bring beneficial reorganizations which might not have otherwise occurred. At least it can be said that Hudson did the decent thing by dying in poverty. He may have ruined countless families, he may have wrecked numerous sensible railway schemes, but he did not last long. Once it was discovered that he had been paying dividends out of capital, and had enriched himself at the expense of his shareholders, his career was finished.

An early and fairly primitive form of corruption in the United States railroad industry was supported by the practice of awarding state grants to railroad construction companies. So great was the public demand for railroads that legislatures, mainly state but occasionally federal, felt compelled to offer financial aid. The builders, having obtained such funds on the basis of inflated estimates, would then build as cheaply as possible and pocket the

difference. When Americans celebrated the completion of the first transcontinental, the railroad they thought was finished was in fact only half-finished, and it would require years to complete the work that the builders had left undone.

Once an individual acquired enough shares to control a railroad, there were different ways in which he could milk it. Watering the stock was a preferred device; this was the secret printing of additional shares that could be sold on the unsuspecting market and which effectively increased the indebtedness of the railroad, while adding nothing to its assets.

Jay Gould, who was fairly typical of the American railroad barons of the late nineteenth century, milked the Erie Railroad in the 1860s before using his gains to finance the acquisition of a commanding number of Union Pacific Railroad (UP) shares. He then caused the UP to pay generous dividends which were not backed by earnings, and sold his shareholding when, in consequence of those dividends, the share price rose high. This gain enabled him to buy the Kansas Pacific (KP), which was one of the UP's competitors. By threatening to reduce Kansas Pacific freight rates and to build a line paralleling one of the UP's, he forced the UP to buy up the KP. He then moved off with his gains to prey on some other railroads.

Gould, and characters like him, enriched themselves while impoverishing the railroads. Apart from the trail of personal ruin

Above left: 'I guess a change of operators is wanted here,' says Uncle Sam in this 1881 cartoon as he takes the railroad barons Vanderbilt (left) and Gould (right) by the scruff of the neck.

Below left: An 1845 cartoon from *Punch,* showing 'King' Hudson receiving homage. The British press was quite rapid in its despatch of Hudson, whose 'rule' was far shorter than that of his American counterparts.

Above right: Jay Gould, creator of the Black Friday financial panic of 1869, and at various times owner and milker of the Erie Railroad. He had a controlling influence over about one fifth of United States railroads and owned the Western Union Telegraph and a New York newspaper. He also inspired, among others, the popular American antipathy to railroad corporations.

Right: 'Jay Gould's Private Bowling Alley' – a cartoonist's comment.

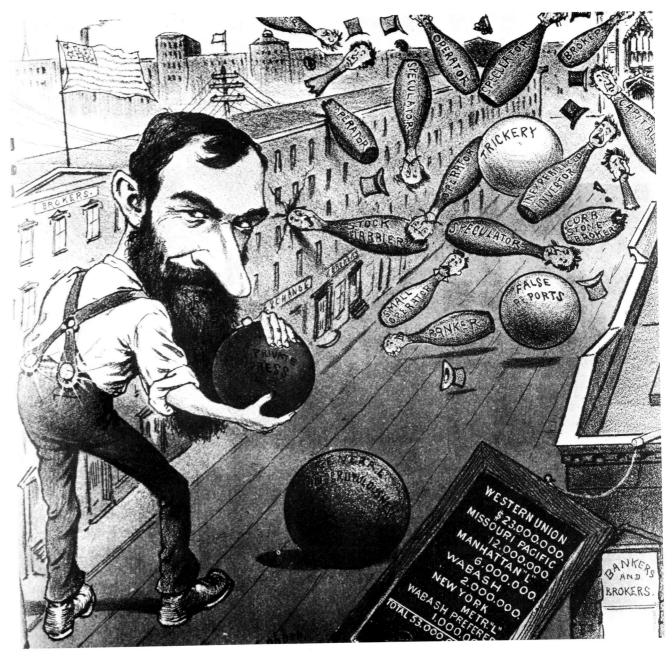

and suicide that they left behind as they devoured the savings or the tax contributions of their fellow-countrymen, their machinations left the United States with thousands of miles of railroad that were badly built, badly located and, in many cases, clearly unwanted. The Nickel Plate Railroad, which was built solely in order to parallel and hence damage the New York Central system, created by those other barons the Vanderbilts, was only one example of a completely unjustified line. Its construction meant that dollars which might have been used to build more useful lines were dissipated to no purpose, and that the New York Central and other lines would be in a weaker financial position when the time came to fight highway competition.

Building unwanted railways for short-term financial gain was not limited to the United States, for in Britain the Direct Portsmouth Line was built by a successful contractor, Thomas Brassey, in the expectation of selling it to the highest bidder among 3 other companies which were already fighting for the Portsmouth traffic. On the whole, Britain and the United States were the most conspicuous victims of this parasitic aggression in which the interests of the railways' shareholders and clients were sacrificed to the greed of unscrupulous operators.

Such abuses became arguments for those who believed that state railways were preferable to private. Certainly the state railways of Belgium and Germany, despite the occasional scandal or misjudgment, represented successful attempts to construct sound railway networks for a minimum capital investment, while in the British Parliament, the young Lloyd George argued that the Prussian State Railways operated far more efficiently than the British companies. Such arguments would be heard over and over again as, one by one, private railway companies were nationalized until the only major private systems left would be in North America and Switzerland.

Opposite page: Crest of the North Midland Railway. This was one of George Hudson's companies and in the 1840s gained notoriety from a wage-cut, leading to the departure of experienced locomotive men and consequently, a serious accident.

Above left: An 1882 cartoonist's nightmare vision of railroad baron Vanderbilt gaining complete control over Americans.

Above: Another Vanderbilt cartoon. By controlling waterways as well as railroads, a man like Vanderbilt could gain a monopoly of long-distance transportation.

Left: In the 1894 Pullman strike, occasioned by a wage reduction at the Pullman Works, President Cleveland despatched troops to break the strikers. This picture, among others, was used to present the troops as protectors of railroad property.

Battle of the Brakes

The first passenger death on a public railway seems to have been that of William Huskisson, the President of the Board of Trade, run down by the *Rocket* at the opening of the Liverpool and Manchester Railway in 1830. It was his own fault. In the United States the first fatality was of the fireman of the locomotive *Best Friend of Charleston* on the South Carolina Railroad, who in an early essay in rationalization tied down the safety valve. The shattered locomotive was later rebuilt and renamed *Phoenix*, but no such resurrection awaited the fireman.

It was not until 1853 that an American railroad accident cost more than 10 lives, and until 1856 the record for the worst accident lay in France, where in 1842 there had been a derailment, followed by a fire, on the Versailles line. The French railways had taken the precaution, from then on abandoned, of locking passengers into their compartments to prevent them jumping out of trains in motion; a practice which caused the incineration of 42 passengers in this disaster.

In Britain, the worst of the nineteenth century accidents was the collapse of the Tay Bridge in 1879, with 74 fatalities. In the United States a burning culvert claimed 82 lives at Chatsworth, Illinois, in 1887, but this was eclipsed by Canada's worst accident, when a Grand Trunk Railroad train plunged over an open drawbridge at St Hilaire, Quebec, taking 88 lives with it. Such high fatalities were rare in accidents, but in 1915 a British record was made when 2 trains of the Caledonian Railway collided, were run down by a third train, and caught fire. The official number of deaths was 227, but even this was not a world record, for in

Above: A head-on collision on the Southern Pacific Railroad at Black Butte. Such accidents, because of the high total momentum, could be catastrophic. Euphemistically known as 'cornfield meets,' they were an inherent peril on single-track routes, relying for safety on human vigilance.

Far left: An accusatory cartoon published on the occasion of the Chatsworth (Illinois) accident of 1887; there were 82 deaths when a train dropped through a burning bridge.

Left: United States semaphore signals at Boston. Attaching signals for both directions to the same gantry, as here, made mistakes more likely.

Right: Cover of a British music-hall song, reflecting the public's concern with railway safety.

Left: Aftermath of a 'cornfield meet' in Colorado, 1896. Despite appearances, this was not a bad accident, as it involved freight trains. The spectators seem to be celebrating rather than mourning, and many of them would be 'souvenir-hunters,' the polite term for looters.

Above: Protecting the public from itself was just as important as protecting passenger trains. In most countries most fatalities did not result from operating accidents. This is an unusual, Australian, warning to the public.

Above right: A British insurance company advertises its services in the 1870s. Much of the traveling public feared railway accidents, and there was a good market for insurance. Some insurance companies, by agreement with the railway company, sold cheap short-term policies through railway ticket offices. Later, a few railways in Europe incorporated a compulsory insurance premium in the price of each ticket, a practice that still survives in the USSR.

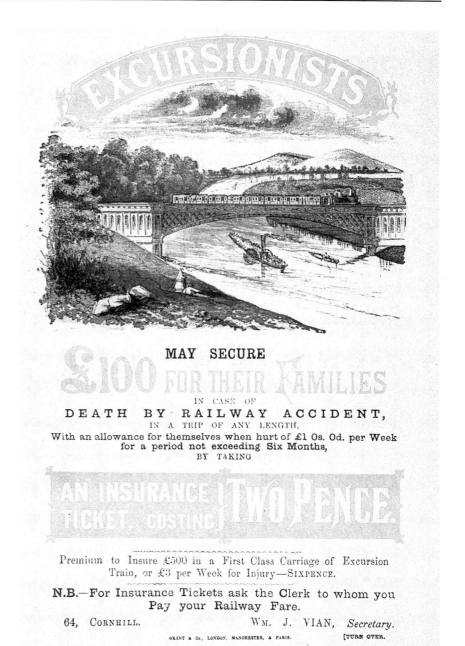

that same year a Mexican train fell into a gorge; 600 were killed.

Improved track more or less kept pace with higher train speeds, so the most frequent accidents were collisions. To reduce these, better signaling and brakes were required, and by the end of the nineteenth century the basic inventions had been achieved and applied to improve these 2 essentials.

Although British, continental, and North American signaling techniques subsequently diverged, in the beginning there were basic similarities. Moving trains were kept separate by signalmen who initially used flags and later, mechanical signals to admit trains into the sections of track they controlled. The time-interval principle was observed, with no train allowed to proceed behind another except after the elapse of a predetermined period of time. In Britain, where lines were usually double-track, this was not hard to apply, although it could only reduce without eliminating the danger of tail-end collisions. In North America, where lines were almost entirely single-track, strict observance of schedules was required.

The electric telegraph enabled a radical improvement to be introduced. On double-track lines the principle of space-interval, much safer than time-interval, was established. Known as the block system, the new technique treated the line between successive signal-men as a block, and no train was allowed to enter one block before its controlling signalman had been informed by the next signalman that the previous train had entered the following block. So long as the signal-men and the locomotive men kept by the rules, a collision was henceforth impossible. In practice, external circumstances might so disturb railwaymen that they broke the rules and caused an accident, but nevertheless the block system was a great step forward.

In the United States the train-order system was made possible by the telegraph. Locomotive men picked up written train orders from despatchers at stations, which had the effect of modifying the regular timetable. So if a northbound train was late, a southbound train could be instructed to take the passing loop at a station farther down the line. Tall semaphore signals outside the despatchers' offices at stations informed locomotive men whether or not there was an order to be picked up.

For multi-track lines the American railroads, as the British, adopted semaphore signals. In Britain these were 2-position, a horizontal arm signifying 'Stop' and a lowered arm meaning 'Proceed.' Later, some railways preferred to raise the arm at 45 degrees to indicate 'Proceed.' Advance warning, or distant, signals were placed at a generous braking distance in front of the 'Stop' signals, to repeat the signal of the latter so that trains would have time to come to a halt. In the United States a similar but more complex set of messages was conveyed by 3-position signals, sometimes 2 to a post.

The first block system was applied between London and Dover in 1851, but spread slowly in Britain. The Camden and Amboy Railroad, in New Jersey, installed the block system in 1865, after a disastrous collision. Both countries used interlocking systems to prevent a signalman inadvertently setting his signals in conflict with those of the adjacent signalman. The first track circuits, in which a train in a block section short-circuited a weak electric current passing through one rail and thereby operated a device that held at 'Stop' the signal controlling entry to that block, were introduced in the 1870s.

The Railway Department of the British Board of Trade recognized quite early the need for a continuous and automatic brake; continuous meant braking power distributed down the train, and automatic really meant fail-safe. In particular, the brake was required to function even when the train was split by a broken coupling.

In the United States, George Westinghouse patented an air brake in 1869, but his really effective version, acting automatically should the train split, appeared in 1872. In the 1880s most American passenger trains were equipped with it, but it was difficult to use on long freight trains because the leading cars were braked long before the rear cars, and this could cause derailments. However, further improvements, and tests conducted on the Burlington Railroad, led to its gradual application to freight trains.

The Westinghouse brake was operated by compressed air, stored in a reservoir and produced by a pump on the locomotive. In Britain railway engineers had perfected a rather similar brake which used atmospheric pressure instead, the brake pump being used to exhaust air from the system. Technically, because it could use higher pressures, the air brake was superior, but it was resisted by many British railways because the vacuum brake seemed quite enough and was already in service. The Board of Trade conducted brake trials at Newark in 1875, and in 1878 the Board put gentle pressure on companies to fit continuous automatic brakes. Compulsion followed in 1889. This harder attitude owed something to the sequel of the Hexthorpe accident in 1887 where 2 trains had collided; the engine-men had been tried for manslaughter but were acquitted after the judge had condemned the unreliable braking system with which they were provided.

But the Board, neither in 1878 nor 1889, specified which system was to be used, so companies took sides in a long 'battle of the brakes' and the end result was that some railways chose the vacuum and others the air brake. This situation was later repeated in South Africa, although for different reasons. As the 2

Left: The Shrewsbury accident of 1907, in which a London and North Western Railway mail train suffered a lethal collision. Several of the casualties were Post-Office workers.

Above right: Britain's worst railway disaster at Quintinshill (Gretna) during World War I. A troop train collided with another passenger train, and a third train ran into the wreckage. Gas from the lighting system helped the flames and there were at least 227 deaths.

Below: A London and North Western Railway publicity card showing a new-style signal-box interior (below right) with small hand levers replacing the massive full-size signal levers normally used.

systems were incompatible, special dual-fitted stock was needed in Britain for continuously braked services over railways using different systems. This really meant that such through services were not operated, the most conspicuous exception being the dual-fitted East Coast passenger trains from London to Scotland in which the southern participant, the Great Northern, used the vacuum brake but the northern participants, the North Eastern and North British railways, used the air brake. This coexistence of incompatible brakes persisted in Britain for another 100 years. It might have all been different if George Westinghouse had not tried to bribe the L & NWR's influential chief mechanical engineer to adopt the air brake. The latter, formerly inclined to prefer the air brake, was a person of extreme or even excessive integrity, and the financial inducement had the opposite effect to that intended.

Luxury on the Line

Although the last 4 decades before World War I saw first-class rail passengers treated to unprecedented privileges and luxuries, this period can also be regarded as one in which many of the older comforts enjoyed by the superior-class passenger were offered to the mass of passengers. In Britain this process had started dramatically when the Midland Railway upgraded third class, allowing its passengers to travel in upholstered comfort on even the fastest of the trains. The soft furnishing of British third-class accommodation was distinctive almost until the present day; indeed, in parts of continental Europe, wooden seats may still be encountered in the lowest class of accommodation, on some secondary lines.

American and British practice continued to diverge in passenger car design. The British still preferred compartments, while the Americans stayed with the open car and central aisle. British sleeping cars were for night use only, unlike those of the Pullman type.

The practice of attaching dining cars to the better trains led, in America, to a fundamental improvement. Access to the diner over the open platform ends of each car was inconvenient and even dangerous, and a better means of crossing from one car to another was sought. The solution, patented in 1887, was invented by a superintendent at the Pullman Works, and was an open metal frame suspended at the end of each car and bearing against a similar frame on the adjoining car. Concertina bellows were attached to it to form a walkway. The previously open end platform was narrowed and enclosed to form a vestibule, making a completely enclosed passage between 2 cars. For more than a decade the 'vestibule train' was the most heavily advertised offering of United States railroads.

Vestibules spread slowly to other countries. In Britain the better longer-distance trains were corridor trains with diners, and these were the first to be so equipped. Another American feature which became popular in Britain for some decades was the raised longitudinal central roof section, or clerestory, which provided extra window area and also a space to suspend the lamps.

Train lighting had developed from nothing, at the start of the Railway Age, to candles, oil lamps, and then gas lamps. Oil and gas were liable to ignite disastrously in accidents, so electric lighting had advantages of safety as well as of smell and convenience. Another fire peril on American railroads had been the car heating stove, typically wood-fired. The provision of steam radiators, using steam piped down the train from the locomotive, was, again, not only a convenience but also a step toward greater

safety. In Britain, steam heating meant the gradual disappearance of the footwarmer. The latter was a metal canister, recharged at main stations, inside which a chemical process produced moderate heat. It survived on Australian secondary lines until the 1980s, enabling diesel locomotives to haul trains designed for steam heat.

In the aftermath of train fires there were often short-lived public demands for all-metal passenger cars, and by 1914 this solution was in sight. The reason, however, was not safety but the increasing cost of the kind of timber needed for making car frames, and the space-saving virtue of steel construction. By 1909 50 percent of American passenger car orders were entirely for all-steel types.

Additional comfort for daytime passengers on long-distance trains in North America was provided by the chair car, or parlor car, which offered more-comfortable seating and often a beverage service. These cars were often placed at the tail-end and were provided with an observation platform. They became a typical feature of the long-distance American train and could also be

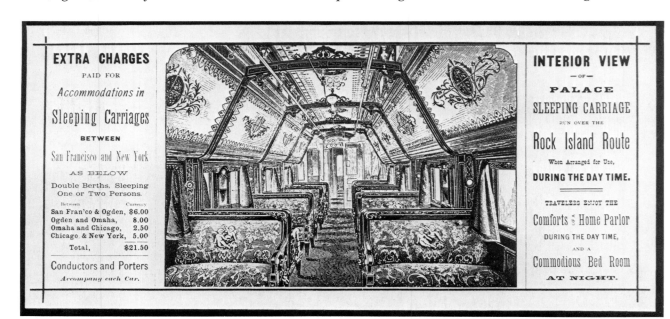

Above: The observation platform, a valued attraction for the North American first-class long-distance passenger.

Left: The Rock Island Railroad advertises a San Francisco to New York service, offered in connection with other railroads.

Above right: An 1883 dining car of the *Orient Express.*

Center right: Accommodation aboard the *Orient Express* in the 1880s.

Right: Interior of the *Orient Express* dining car.

Left: Inside a Union Pacific Railroad parlor car of the early 1900s.

Below left: Interior of a dining car built about 1910 for the Great Central Railway's London extension.

Below: The King's bedroom in the British royal saloon of 1903.

Right: The excursion train became a feature of society from the mid-nineteenth century. This advertisement from Canada is typical.

Below right: The *North Coast Limited*, pride of the Northern Pacific Railroad, in about 1900.

Below far right: The Canadian Pacific Railway proclaims the forthcoming service through to Vancouver.

found in Australia, which adopted several other American features. In Britain and other countries where train journeys were relatively short, they were very rare. Another North American feature was the business car; a vehicle, usually privately owned, that provided home comforts for those rich enough to own one. Most of them, including those used by railroad managers to tour their lines, were fairly simple, but there were others that were expensively and ostentatiously fitted out. One financier even had solid gold water pipes, said to be more economical than copper as they did not require polishing.

The cars provided for royalty were also quite luxurious and several have found their way into railway museums. Queen Victoria, apart from having her own royal train in Britain, kept 2 royal vehicles in France, at Calais, which she could use for her continental travels. Her son King Edward VII did the same, and while using one in Belgium narrowly escaped death from an assassin's bullet.

Train Services

Although almost all railways earned more revenue from freight than from passengers, progress in freight services was less noticeable, usually consisting of a steady increase in scale, with progressively longer trains, bigger freight cars and, after the introduction of continuous brakes, an increase of average speeds. Passenger services at the end of the nineteenth century benefitted from a general acceleration not only on the competition-orientated American and British railways, but also in continental Europe and Australia. The average speed of trains was highest in Britain, overall, but the United States claimed to have the fastest trains in the world.

In North America the most dramatic competition was between the Reading and the Pennsylvania railroads for the Philadelphia to Atlantic City traffic. The rail distance was 55 miles for one company and 58 for the other, and in 1899, after 2 years of competitive scheduling, both lines were allowing 55 minutes for the trip. In effect, this meant that for 50 miles or so the trains averaged around 65mph, which was a speed no British railway could match over that distance, although the London and South Western Railway did have a 60mph timing over 15 miles.

Elsewhere in the United States speeds were rising from their low averages of the 1880s. In that decade, only a handful of trains averaged more than 40mph, and these were mainly confined to the Jersey City to Philadelphia, and Baltimore to Washington services. Chicago was 25 hours from New York and 14 hours from St Paul. But at the end of the century, the Chicago and North Western Railroad was running to St Paul in 10 hours, while 2 competing New York to Chicago overnight trains, the New York Central's *Twentieth Century Limited* and the Pennsylvania Railroad's *Pennsylvania Special* (predecessor of the *Broadway Limited*) brought the New York to Chicago timing down in 1902

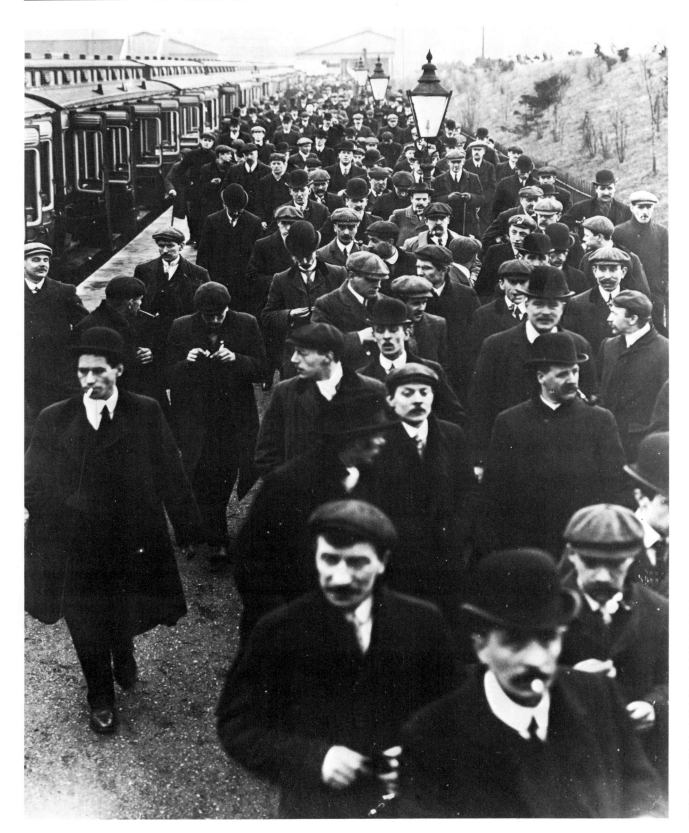

Left: A GWR football special unloads its passengers in 1908. Such services, utilizing rolling stock outside peak hours, could be a good bargain both for the railways and their passengers.

Above right: One of the Midland Railway's best trains in 1911, composed of 6-wheel and 8-wheel vehicles. To segregate its slow-moving coal traffic from its passenger services, the MR favored multi-track main lines.

Right: The August 1910 holiday season at Paddington Station, London.

to 20 hours, which in 1905 was reduced to 18 hours. After this peak performance, however, there was a relapse to slightly longer schedules.

The New York Central was also the operator of the *Empire State Express*, introduced in 1892 between New York and Buffalo; a distance of almost 440 miles. Excluding 2 stops for locomotive change, the schedule allowed 426 minutes. As with most fast trains, the load was small, typically only 4 cars, and it was this train, hauled by the celebrated No 999, which was said to have covered a mile in 32 seconds.

The practice of naming trains that were regarded as deserving special public attention became widespread in the United States, common in Britain, but less noticeable elsewhere. One of the earliest names was that of the *Irish Mail*, which began running from London to Holyhead in 1848. Providing the mail service to the then British city of Dublin, it was required by the Post Office to maintain quite rigorous timings; as early as 1860 it was averaging 42mph. To help this train along, the technique of picking up and setting down mailbags at speed was developed, a practice that later came to the United States. By 1900 this train was ave-

raging more than 50mph over the 265 miles, with only 1 intermediate stop for engine changing.

The Great Western Railway passenger services were perhaps the most progressive in Britain at the end of the century. The GWR had introduced the first side-corridor train in 1891, and proceeded to accelerate its fast trains and introduce others; the final abolition of its broad gauge in 1892 had evidently infused a dynamic spirit into its management. Its best London to Bristol service covered the 118 miles in 2¼ hours, and in 1904 it introduced its *Cornish Riviera Limited*, with a grueling schedule over the heavily graded main line through Devon.

Most of the larger British towns were served by 2 or more companies, and between any 2 towns there was usually more than 1 route. Competitive pressures drove companies to provide faster services, so the increase of average speeds, unlike in the United States, was a process that lasted up to World War I. The Caledonian Railway, for example, faced with competition from the North British, was running many 50mph trains as early as 1906, and also a 60mph train over the 32 miles from Perth to Forfar. In 1888 and 1895 there had been the 'Races' from London to

Left: A pre-World War I poster praising the East Coast route to Scotland.

Above right and above far right: The 2 sides of an advertising card extolling the West Coast route to Scotland, and probably giving the would-be passenger rather more information than was needed.

Right: The Victorian Railways' *Melbourne Express* near Benalla in 1910. Like other Australian railways, VR used British designs of locomotive, although some of them were built in its own workshops.

Scotland, in which for a few days the West Coast companies and East Coast companies sought to undercut each other's timings. Very high, often unprecedented speeds were achieved in these spontaneous bursts of intense competition, although it is doubtful if they were enjoyed by the passengers; the latter probably stayed away if they could, and there is no doubt that the trains were reduced in size day by day and were little more than 100 tons on the last days. No disasters ensued, but risks were taken.

Another hotly competitive route was between Plymouth and London on the days that transatlantic liners berthed at Plymouth. Both the GWR and its rival the London and South Western ran fast 'Ocean Mails' connecting with the ships. It was in the course of one such race to London in 1906 that the L & SW Railway's 'Ocean Mail' hurtled off the rails on the Salisbury curve, killing 24 passengers.

In continental Europe, too, trains were becoming faster. In

1900 it was possible to cover the 540 miles from Paris to Marseilles at an average speed of 45mph, although this was in a luxury train at a fare 4 times the third-class rate; for the ordinary passenger there was a train averaging 40mph. In other countries, whose railways were not built for speed, the accent was put on comfort. Russia had its Trans-Siberian express, which included a piano among its attractions, while in South Africa, the *Union Limited*, connecting with the British mailboat, and the predecessor of the *Blue Train*, had its beginnings in 1903.

Australia, in this period, was enjoying a foretaste of interstate travel. After 1873 it was possible to journey by train between Sydney and Melbourne, with a break of gauge at Albury, and the two railways concerned, Victorian Railways and the New South Wales Government Railways, made a special effort with their Melbourne Cup race trains. In 1891 they were able to provide Pullman sleeping cars for these 26-berth vehicles, which

included a 2-berth ladies' cabin at one end. They also provided the so-called 'lavatory carriages,' in which washrooms were made available for the first time to second-class passengers. By 1908 2 regular daily trains were running from Sydney to Albury, the *Limited* and the *Express*, and the timings required average speeds of 45mph on some sections. This route seemed to have a glowing future, and this expectation was not dimmed when the first airmail flight was organized from Sydney to Melbourne in summer 1914; the intrepid aviator required no less than 2¼ days to cover the course.

While railway companies were introducing long-distance trains that were faster and usually heavier than their predecessors, they were also encouraging the growth of short-distance traffic. Commuter services had been developing for several decades, aided by special reduced fares for workers. The trains were frequent, and stopped at most or all of the stations on their

Left: London and South Western Railway trains arriving in London, in 1912. The newly rebuilt side of Waterloo Station is pictured, but part of the old side is visible in the background.

Below: The *Pennsylvania Limited* of the Pennsylvania Railroad in about 1899. Predecessor of the *Broadway Limited*, this train was run in direct competition with trains of several other companies for the New York to Chicago traffic.

Below right: Payday for the Union Pacific construction workers. The nearest car, under armed guard, carries the money.

comparatively short runs. They did much to change society, enabling people to live outside the cities in which they worked and instead to commute in, on a daily basis, to their places of employment. But they were often unprofitable, because they had sharp traffic peaks, between which the rolling stock was unproductive. Moreover, the intensity of these services meant that extra tracks had to be laid for them. So 4-track lines out of London were created, and this trackage was also required in the approaches to a few other cities. In the United States much single-track line was doubled for the same reason, and often resignaled too. The process was not confined to these countries. Melbourne, Sydney, Calcutta and Johannesburg soon needed multi-track approaches, while cities such as Paris and Berlin acquired intricate railway networks.

The Transcontinentals

The first American transcontinental route, despite the financial scandals that accompanied it, was an unquestioned success. It was evidently destined to be profitable; it was opening up for development vast tracts in the West as far as the Pacific, and for a time it did help to give Americans a sense of nationhood. The United States was a wide country, and there was room for more transcontinentals. Among these were the Atchison, Topeka and Santa Fe Railroad, which by 1889 linked Chicago to the Pacific through Colorado and Kansas, having almost fought its way over the Raton Pass into New Mexico against the militant opposition of the Denver and Rio Grande Western Railroad (D & RGW). The D & RGW Railroad later joined with the Western Pacific at Salt Lake City to form another route to the Pacific. Then there was what became the Southern Pacific's line from New Orleans through Texas to Los Angeles. In the far north, the Canadian-born James Hill, not the worst of the railroad barons, managed to build 2 transcontinentals, the Great Northern (GN) and the Northern Pacific (NP), both running west to Seattle but taking different routes. Hill also controlled the Chicago, Burlington and Quincy Railroad, and naturally routed traffic originating on his GN and NP over that line. The Burlington's rival, the Milwaukee Railroad, to overcome this disadvantage built its own extension to the Pacific, thereby finishing the last American transcontinental. Its completion in 1909 was only 7 years in advance of the Panama Canal, which took traffic from all the transcontinentals.

Nation-building was a conspicuous objective of the Canadian Pacific Railway (CP), for it was built to encourage British Columbia to join a proposed confederation of Britain's North American colonies rather than one day become part of the United States. The CP Railway was a difficult line to build, facing not only the Rockies but also expanses of swamp and muskeg around Lake Superior. But with strong financial and political support in London, setbacks were never allowed to kill it; the first through train from Montreal to the Pacific at Vancouver ran in 1886, taking 139 hours for the trip. Two decades later a competing line, the Canadian Northern, was under way and in 1915 was able to open a Quebec to Vancouver service. Moreover, a third route of very high construction standards was also initiated. This consisted of a government project, the National Transcontinental Railway, which was laid from New Brunswick, over the new Quebec Bridge, and from there through virgin country to Winnipeg, where it linked with the Grand Trunk Pacific, which was building a line through the Rockies to Prince Rupert on the Pacific. This 3543-mile route was completed in 1919, just in time to form part of the new Canadian National Railways, the government corporation formed to rescue Canada from the consequences of excessive railroad construction.

The Canadian Pacific was one of the inspirations behind the construction of the Trans-Siberian Railway by the Russian government, whose purpose was to consolidate the Russian hold

on Siberia and the Pacific provinces by developing the eastern
economy, supporting a fleet on the Pacific, and extending
Russian political and economic influence in China. To save
mileage, part of it was laid across Manchuria, over Chinese territory, and was known as the Chinese Eastern Railway (CE). Political sharp practice soon resulted in a Russian-owned branch line,
the South Manchuria Railway, dropping south from the CE Railway to Port Arthur, a Chinese seaport which became a Russian
naval base. With such obvious expansionist purposes, it was
hardly surprising that the Trans-Siberian would be immediately
engulfed in the Russo-Japanese War, after which St Petersburg
was obliged to give up Port Arthur and the South Manchuria
Railway.

Another political transcontinental, the Cape to Cairo Railway,
was overtaken by events and never completed. It was the concept
of Cecil Rhodes, and envisaged joining the South African railways to the Egyptian Cairo to Luxor line by a route crossing
Africa from south to north and consolidating British influence
throughout its length. It was routed through Bechuanaland so as
to avoid the Transvaal, which was then the anti-British South
African Republic. It passed through Bulawayo, crossed the Zam-
bezi by the celebrated Victoria Falls Bridge, but did not progress
beyond Northern Rhodesia.

It was probably World War I and its aftermath that ended the
Cape to Cairo dream. The Trans-Australian Railway was actually
opened at the height of that conflict, in 1917. It was undertaken by

Below: Sacramento yard of the
Central Pacific Railroad. The stock of
rails on the right suggests that
construction is still underway,
making 1869 the most likely date for
this picture.

Right: Two Medecine Bridge of the
Great Northern Railroad, a superb
example of timber construction. As
the date is 1891 and the locomotive
is cautiously pushing a boxcar ahead
of it, this picture probably shows a
trial run over the newly completed
structure.

Below right: Section men with their
hand trolley on the Canadian Pacific
Railway in British Columbia, just
before the line was opened.

a federal organization, Commonwealth Railways, following the federation of the Australian colonies in 1901. Its main purpose, as that of the Canadian Pacific, was to tie the most distant state in with the rest of the new nation. It linked existing railheads in Western Australia and South Australia and was 1051 miles long. The choice of the 4-foot 8½-inch gauge, even though the 2 terminal states had systems of 3 feet 6 inches and 5 feet 3 inches res-pectively, was intended to be a first step in standardizing the Australian railway gauge. It was a difficult line to build and to operate, because of water shortage, but natural obstacles were so rare that 297 successive miles of it could be laid perfectly straight across the Nullarbor Plain (the world's longest straight stretch), while the absence of stiff gradients enabled a single locomotive to haul heavy trains.

The Narrow-Gauge Railway

As railway networks expanded, a point was reached when the main towns were served, but smaller and less prosperous communities remained isolated. Evidently, a cheaper type of railway was needed and the narrow gauge seemed the best solution, being considerably cheaper to build.

A big advantage of the narrow gauge, with its acceptance of sharp curves, was its ability to clasp the contours of a landscape. This meant that expensive earthworks and tunneling could be largely eliminated. Since rolling stock was smaller, it cost less, and the small size was no deterrent if heavy traffic was not anticipated. The narrow gauge did, however, present a problem; it could not exchange cars with adjacent, full-size railways. This was not serious for passengers, who were able to change trains at junctions in the usual way, but it did mean that freight had to be transhipped.

A definition of a narrow-gauge railway is not always easy, for one man's narrow gauge is another man's standard gauge. In the British colony of Sierra Leone, for example, the railway network was of the 2-foot 6-inch gauge; a scale that would be regarded as tiny in most parts of the world. In South Africa, the mainline railways are of 3 feet 6 inches, which would be regarded as a narrow gauge in many countries. In Japan the standard gauge was 3 feet 6 inches until a network of 4-foot 8½-inch gauge lines was built.

Two British-built narrow-gauge lines had a great influence in popularizing the idea. The Ffestiniog Railway in Wales, laid for

Above left: The Austro-Hungarian Empire favored narrow-gauge railways and this line to Sarajevo, pictured after it became part of Yugoslav State Railways, was not converted to standard gauge until after World War II.

Left: One of many 3-foot-gauge lines in Colorado converted to standard gauge. This picture shows the last narrow-gauge train leaving Climax over mixed-gauge track.

Above right: The narrow-gauge transporter, still used in Central Europe, enables standard-gauge freight cars to move over narrow-gauge trackage. This picture was taken at Wolkenstein in Germany.

Right: A 2-foot 6-inch gauge passenger train climbs out of Garsten, Austria.

the transportation of quarried slate from the mountains down to
the sea, was able to carry very heavy traffic even though it was
only of 2-foot gauge. It was particularly noteworthy after 1870,
when it began to use Fairlie's patent double-ended locomotives,
designed especially for high-power outputs over sharply curved
track.

The Barsi Light Railway in India, perhaps equally influential,
was no short line, being 115 miles long. Of 2-foot 6-inch gauge, it
was constructed by E Calthrop, a theoretician of the narrow
gauge. He used light rail, accepted a 15mph speed limit, designed
locomotives with short wheelbases, low axle weights, but considerable power, and used high-capacity all-metal freight cars of
15-ton capacity; in fact, his freight cars were technically in
advance of those used by most of the British mainline railways.
After the Barsi line was built, Calthrop's reputation grew, and it
was on his advice that the government of Victoria in Australia
began to lay a series of 2-foot 6-inch gauge lines to supplement
the mainline 5-foot 3-inch gauge system.

The narrow gauge also became popular in India and South
Africa for localities too poor to justify big investment. In South
Africa the narrow-gauge lines in Natal did much to encourage development, while the 177-mile Port Elizabeth to Avontuur line
opened up a rich fruit-growing area.

In the United States there was a 'narrow-gauge fever' in the
1870s and 1880s. In Colorado, both the Colorado Central and the
Denver and Rio Grande Western chose the 3-foot gauge as the
largest practicable for that mountainous region. By 1883 the D &
RGW was running trains over a 770-mile heavily graded main
line between Denver and Ogden. Although in later years it was

steadily changed to standard gauge, the D & RGW set a fashion, and by 1900 only 6 states were without narrow-gauge lines. Most were of 3-foot gauge, but there were others. In Maine, the Sandy River and Rangeley Lakes Railroad had a 2-foot gauge network of over 100 miles.

France and Belgium also built narrow-gauge lines, the meter gauge being preferred. Austria, Germany and Switzerland used a variety of gauges and many of their narrow-gauge lines are still in use. The narrow gauge was also suitable for non-public railways, especially agricultural railways which, in the period before the highway vehicle, began to appear on plantation-style, specialized, landholdings. The Decauville portable light railway, developed in France, was a 2-foot gauge system used by many large farms in France, especially in the beet-growing areas. In many other parts of the world, including Queensland in Australia, and the East and West Indies, 2-foot gauge sugar-cane lines, working only during the harvest season, were used.

The British were great proponents of the narrow gauge overseas, but were rather reluctant to employ it at home, preferring the light railway concept. The light railway is one where cheapness is obtained by employing lower constructional and operating standards while retaining, usually, the normal gauge. In return for allowing such railways to operate, the government imposed certain safety regulations that would have been intolerable for normal lines operating heavy trains at high speeds. The most important was a very low speed limit, which was necessary in view of the absence of signaling systems and of gates at highway crossings.

Improving the Locomotive

After 1875 steam locomotive development took 2 directions, those of consolidation and innovation. Consolidation meant the building of locomotives incorporating the advances of the previous decades, progress being measured by a steady increase in size, with its corollary of new wheel arrangements to bear the increased weight. Innovation meant radical technical advance, to improve efficiency or to increase power without a proportionate increase of length or axle weight, both of which were restricted by limitations imposed by the track.

The 4-4-0 wheel arrangement, so long dominant in North America, was eventually succeeded there by the 2-6-0 and the 4-6-0, both of which could provide more total weight on driving wheels and so more adhesion to allow the application of greater power without wheelslip. In Britain the 4-4-0 would linger, some modern examples actually being built in the 1930s, but there, too, the type was superseded for passenger work by the 'Atlantic' 4-4-2 and the 4-6-0, with the 4-6-2 making a cautious appearance before World War I. In America the 'Pacific,' or 4-6-2, arrived earlier and was soon adopted by many railroads. Its highest manifestation was probably the 'K4' type of the Pennsylvania Railroad, which produced a very high power output on test and was used for the Railroad's faster passenger trains over several decades.

The 4-6-2 had the advantage that the low rear axle allowed a wide firebox to be fitted. This, in turn, increased the all-important grate area, which determined the sustainable power output. The 4-6-0 had a narrow firebox, which is perhaps why it did not have a long life as a top passenger locomotive in the United States. In Britain, however, and in those countries like Australia and India which closely followed British practice, the 4-6-0 had a long reign; in some cases the limiting rear axle was moved well back behind the firebox, producing an irregular spacing of the driving wheels that was also to be seen in other wheel arrangements. The 4-6-0 did have one advantage over the 4-6-2, in that a

greater proportion of its weight was on the driving wheels, so it was less prone to slip. The GWR stayed with the 4-6-0 right up to the end of steam while the South African railways, faced with the 1 in 40 (2 percent) gradient over the Hex River Pass and the long 1 in 66 climbs of the Durban line, used the 4-6-0, and also the 4-8-0, for many years.

For freight work the British railways would continue to build simple inside-cylinder 0-6-0s for many more years, but 0-8-0s were built for mineral traffic, and later 2-8-0s. The latter had the advantage that they could use the same components as the 4-6-0, just as, in America, the popular 2-8-2 freight locomotive could use standard parts shared with the 4-6-2. In America the 2-10-0 and 2-10-2 soon made their appearances on lines with stiff gradients or heavy trains, but 10 coupled wheels were regarded as excessive in Britain.

The British railways, because of their shorter distances, were large users of tank locomotives which, because they did not have tenders, could run in either direction and therefore did not need to be turned at the end of their usually short runs. One variety of tank locomotive, the Forney tank, did become popular in the United States. This carried its water not in side tanks but behind the cab, and was used for suburban workings.

Above left: Dabhoi, a busy station on the extensive 2-foot 6-inch gauge system of India's Western Railway.

Left: On the Cuzco to Santa Ana Railway in Peru. This 3-foot-gauge line, built by American engineers and resembling United States narrow-gauge railways is pictured near Cuzco. The ability of the narrow gauge to hug the land is shown clearly, here.

Above right: The first British 4-6-0 was the 1894 'Jones Goods' class of the Highland Railway, pictured here.

Right: British railways, with their short distances, made great use of tank locomotives. This is one of the London, Brighton and South Coast Railway's 'Terriers,' used in passenger service for many decades.

Left: One of the last Shay locomotives to remain in use, No 508 of the Bolivian State Railways. This picture shows the right-hand side, where the cylinders and gears are located.

Right: No 1223, a late nineteenth century Pennsylvania Railroad passenger locomotive, possibly representing the ultimate development of the American 4-4-0.

Below: A Garratt locomotive in passenger service, passing through ostrich country. The Garratt locomotive, producing high power but suited for light, curving, track, was bought in large numbers by the South African Railways.

The low thermal efficiency of the steam locomotive, with most of the energy potential of the coal going unused up the chimney, began to concern engineers as the railways' coal bills grew. A method of improving matters was compounding, in which steam used by a cylinder was led not to the chimney but to a second low-pressure cylinder where it could give up more of its power. Various permutations were used. On the British Midland Railway, which produced a successful 4-4-0 compound early in the twentieth century, there was a high-pressure cylinder between the frames, exhausting into 2 outside low-pressure cylinders. On the London and North Western Railway whose compounds were generally unsuccessful, there were 2 small high-pressure outside cylinders, exhausting into a wide low-pressure cylinder in the middle. In Germany and Russia, in particular, the outside-cylinder 'cross-compound' became popular. This had a small high-pressure cylinder on one side and a big low-pressure cylinder on the other. The system was not very suitable for the faster engines, because it was impossible to equalize the power output of the 2 cylinders. Despite this disadvantage, the cross-compound locomotive was built in large numbers, the Russians having an 0-8-0 version which finally totaled about 8000 engines; a world record at the time.

Above left: Three British-built 2-8-0 locomotives of the New South Wales Government Railways. The 2-8-0 became a British favorite for mineral traffic, and these Australian examples were used for coal haulage.

Left: A United States-style 4-6-0 of the Canadian Pacific hauls a passenger train past the Ottawa parliament buildings.

Right: An 'E' class 0-10-0 of the Soviet Railways. This design, introduced in 1912, became the world's most numerous locomotive class, with about 12,000 units built.

In America the Vauclain compound was briefly popular, and included the record-breaking 4-4-2s of the Reading Railroad. In the Vauclain scheme there were 4 outside cylinders, with the high-pressure ones placed directly above the low-pressure. But with ruggedness, reliability, and simplicity being regarded on American railroads as more important than coal and water economy, compounding was not especially popular in the United States. It was developed to the highest degree in France, aided possibly by the better technical training of French locomotive men, who could be trusted to get the best out of these more complicated machines. The du Bousquet layout became the most popular in France; this had 4 cylinders, the high-pressure ones being outside.

Meanwhile, Wilhelm Schmidt of the Prussian State Railways was developing another line of attack; the locomotive superheater. This was a bank of steam elements which led the steam, on its way from the boiler to the cylinders, through a reheating process that raised its temperature far enough to prevent condensation when it entered the cylinders. By eliminating condensation, greater power was obtained from a given quantity of steam. It was soon found that superheating produced economies as good as compounding, and by a much cheaper method. This is one reason why the British railways did not use the compounding process for long, even though trials held on the Midland Railway suggested that although a superheated engine was more efficient than a compound in most conditions, a superheated compound was the most efficient of all.

One of the earlier French advocates of compounding was Anatole Mallet, who designed a type of articulated locomotive to exploit it. This later became known as the 'Mallet' locomotive and it had a boiler which was attached to a power unit (that is, cylinders and driving wheels) at the rear but merely rested on the second, forward, power unit, which was therefore free to swivel independently from the rest of the locomotive. This enabled a larger number of driving wheels to be used, thereby keeping the critical axle weight low in relation to the weight available for adhesion. The weakness of the Mallet locomotive was the flexible steampipes and steam joints needed to connect the swiveling forward unit with the boiler. By making the forward unit the low-pressure part of a compound locomotive, this problem of steam escape was largely overcome.

In France and Germany the Mallet locomotive took the form of tank locomotives for sharply curved lines, typically narrow-gauge. In the United States, the Mallet idea was adopted on a large scale for heavy freight locomotives, enabling the railroads to go beyond the conventional 2-10-0 and 2-10-2; although the Union Pacific did use some 4-12-2 engines, 12 driving wheels in a rigid frame were really too many for curved track. The first American Mallet was an 0-6-6-0 built for the Baltimore and Ohio Railroad, which was so successful that other railroads began to order larger versions. In 1920 the Virginian Railway would reach the limit of the compound Mallet, with a series of 2-10-10-2 locomotives in which the low-pressure cylinders were 4 feet in diameter; cylinders bigger than this were impossible to accom-

Left: A 4-6-4 suburban tank locomotive used by the Western Australian Government Railways for services out of Perth.

Below left: A Shay locomotive takes water at La Paz, Bolivia.

Right: One of the GWR 'Star' class engines at Swansea in South Wales, toward the end of its life in the 1950s.

Below: One of the 8th class freight locomotives of the Cape Government (later South African) Railways. This was of the 4-8-0 wheel arrangement, long a favorite in South Africa.

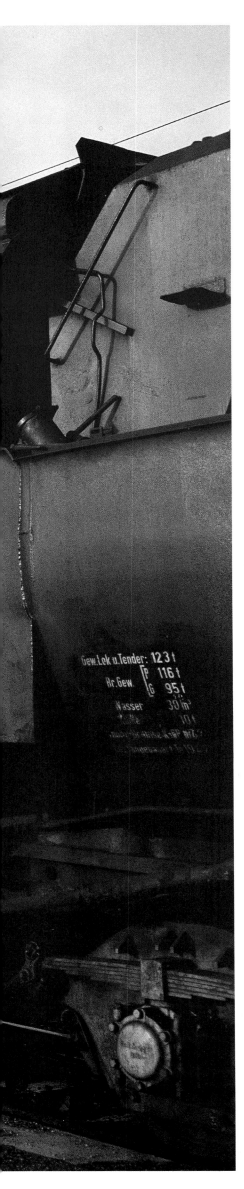

Left: One of the last surviving Prussian 'P8' 4-6-0 locomotives, photographed in 1967 in southern Germany.

Above: An official photograph of a 'P8' 4-6-0 in Royal Prussian State Railways finish. About 3800 units of this class were built, making it the world's most numerous passenger locomotive type. War and reparations took many units to the railways of France, Belgium and central and eastern Europe. Being uncomplicated and with light axle-weight, it was a very useful design, and some units survived into the 1980s in Romania. The characteristic Prussian chimney extension is plainly visible in this photograph.

modate, so subsequent more powerful Mallets were Mallet simples (that is, non-compound, so all cylinders were high-pressure). Interesting but not very successful variants of the Mallet included a series built by Baldwin in which greater flexibility was obtained by actually using a jointed boiler, and the 'Triplex' of the Erie Railroad, which had 3 power units, the extra one carrying the tender.

The British engineer Herbert Garratt devised a successful alternative to the Mallet. The 'Garratt' locomotive was also articulated, but the boiler was slung between, rather than above, the 2 power units, and both of the latter could swivel. This produced a type that was more flexible than the Mallet and also had ample space below the boiler in which a firebox and ashpan, with really good air circulation, could be fitted. The Garratt locomotive was first supplied to a narrow-gauge line in Tasmania, but was later built in large numbers, especially for railways in the British Empire. A Soviet commentator later wrote that the British had invented the Garratt to save the wages of locomotive crew in their colonies; the grain of truth in this was that the Garratt could be regarded as 2 locomotives driven by a single crew.

South African Railways were enthusiastic users of Garratt locomotives, and in the early 1920s held comparative trials between Garratt, Mallet, and conventional units. In these, as could have been expected, the Garratt performed best, thanks largely to its efficient boiler. Despite its advantages, however, the Garratt was never bought for North American railroads. The latter preferred to stick with the Mallet, thereby exhibiting the kind of managerial inertia that was later to prove so costly.

Just as the Garratt locomotive patents were taken up by one particular builder, Beyer Peacock of Manchester, so was another innovatory concept, the 'Shay' locomotive, adopted by the American Lima Locomotive Works. Ephraim Shay designed this locomotive to work on rough forestry lines, where the rails were light, badly laid, and sharply curved. This very successful type had its cylinders placed vertically on one side of the boiler. They drove a crankshaft which was coupled to rotating shafts. These in turn, by means of bevel gears, transmitted their rotary motion to the wheels on that, right-hand, side of the engine. The wheels were in two 4-wheel trucks, which were free to rotate, so sharp curves were no problem, while the long space between the 2 trucks spread the locomotive's weight. It was only the decline of the United States logging industry which brought an end to Shay production in 1945. The last surviving Shays were in Bolivia, Taiwan and the Philippines, and were active in the latter at least until the mid-1980s.

Railroad Electrification

Although it would not be until the 1920s that the really big railway electrification schemes would be started, by 1900 the major technical problems had been solved and the main obstacle to electrification was the high cost of the initial equipment. Although burning coal in a generating station and using the electricity for traction provided more horsepower per ton of coal than the conventional steam locomotive, the cost of the generating plant, sub-stations, and the conductor rails or overhead conductors to feed the locomotives was prohibitive except where there was a high volume of traffic over which these capital costs could be spread. Also, at a time of rapid technical progress there was an understandable reluctance to embark on electrification schemes which, within a few years, would be obsolete. However, exceptions were made where there were short lengths of line which, perhaps because of the heavy gradients or long tunnels, were especially difficult for steam traction.

The German von Siemens operated a small electric locomotive at the Berlin Trade Exhibition of 1879, but Volk's Railway in Brighton, England, was the first public electric railway. This short sea-front line, which still exists, used cars similar to streetcars, drawing current at low voltage from a third rail. In the United States in the 1880s, 2 electric locomotives were built by Leo Daft, and van der Poele showed how current could be conducted to the train by an overhead wire. Frank Sprague also developed the idea of the multiple-unit train, in which several electric motors along the train could be controlled from one cab.

In 1890 one of the London underground railways replaced steam locomotives with electric, and 5 years later the Baltimore and Ohio built an electrified line at Baltimore connecting its western and northern main lines. The city authorities had rejected a proposal for an elevated line, so a tunnel was dug instead. This was electrified because of the smoke problem, and electric locomotives hauled the trains, complete with their temporarily inactive steam locomotives, through the underground section. This electrification was imitated by several other North American lines. In New York the city authorities, tired of the smoke nuisance from the New York Central trains using the Park Avenue tunnel to reach Grand Central Terminal, prohibited the

THE NEW AND THE OLD: A RACE BETWEEN THE ELECTRIC AND STEAM LOCOMOTIVES OF THE NEW YORK CENTRAL AND HUDSON RIVER RAILROAD, BOTH THE LATEST TYPES

use of steam traction south of the Harlem River. The New York Central decided to electrify and, unlike the Baltimore and Ohio, which used overhead conductors, it opted for a third rail, carrying 600V DC current; the 35 locomotives did have a tiny pantograph, but this was only to pick up overhead current at places where track turnouts interrupted the third rail.

The New Haven Railroad, which shared the tracks into Grand Central, was not content with merely electrifying for a few miles,

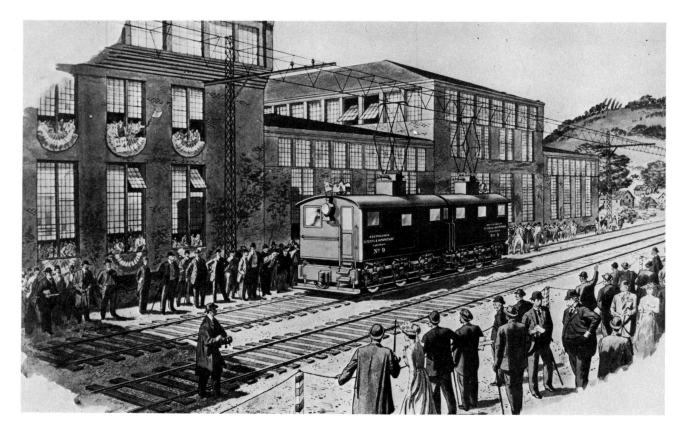

Above: The *Scientific American* commemorates the introduction of electric traction on the New York Central Railroad.

Left: A single-phase AC locomotive built by Baldwin and Westinghouse in 1904, from which developed locomotives supplied for the New Haven Railroad electrification.

Above right: A Baltimore and Ohio Railroad electric locomotive hauling a steam train through the Baltimore Tunnel.

Right: Volk's Electric Railway at Brighton, England, the earliest public electric railway.

and decided to convert its main line out of New York as far as New Haven; this 72-mile stretch was ready by 1914, using the 11,000V AC system offered by the Westinghouse Corporation. This voltage was also chosen by the Norfolk and Western Railroad when it electrified its steeply graded line through the Elkhorn Tunnel in West Virginia. Meanwhile, the Milwaukee Railroad had begun to electrify difficult sections of its new main line, and the Canadian Northern Railway, which had envisaged electrification from the start, was burrowing through Mount Royal to provide an outlet to the north of Montreal. The tunnel was completed in 1918 and the 2400V DC overhead system, designed by General Electric, was later extended to permit the introduction of electric commuter services.

In Britain, by World War I, several railways had begun to experiment with short electrifications, and several different, incompatible, systems were in use. In 1904 2 third-rail 600V schemes were started; the Lancashire and Yorkshire Railway's 37-mile Liverpool to Southport commuter line, and the North Eastern Railway's Newcastle scheme, whose 32 miles were expected to carry heavy freight as well as passenger traffic. It was already realized that high-voltage systems were potentially more economical, but they presented technical problems. The Midland Railway's 10-mile Lancaster to Heysham electrification was at 6600V AC, and so was the London, Brighton and South Coast's 8-mile South London scheme. During the war the L & NWR's 630V scheme, using third and fourth rails, came into use in the north London suburbs, and so did the Lancashire and Yorkshire's 1200V third-rail Manchester to Bury project, and the London to Wimbledon 650V third-rail scheme of the London and South Western Railway. It was the latter, even then not the technically best system, which was destined to expand after the war.

In France, a variety of systems was tried in the south, and in 1900 the Paris to Orleans Railway began a 1500V overhead-conductor scheme from the capital to the southwest. This did not progress far before the war, but it was to be the nucleus for France's first major mainline electrification. In Germany, where the steam locomotive was well-entrenched as a very reliable performer burning cheap local fuel, electrification was not much favored. Overhead conductors were frowned upon by the military authorities, who argued that a break in the wire could bring trains to a standstill for many miles, and this would be a weak link in mobilization plans. However, the Prussian State Railways did begin a 15,000V AC project through the Silesian mountains which was completed in 1928, only to be dismantled and taken east, lock, stock and barrel, by the victorious Russians in 1945.

Above left: One of 4 locomotives supplied by General Electric for the Great Northern Railroad's Cascade Tunnel electrification of 1909.

Left: One of several types of electric locomotive used for the NYC Railroad's electrification out of New York.

Above right: A German electric locomotive built in 1909 for service in the Bavarian mountains and still at work in the early 1980s.

Right: A pair of 'box-cab' electric locomotives built by English Electric in the 1920s and still used by Canadian National Railways for Montreal commuter services in the 1980s.

PART 3

FEELING THE STRAIN:
1914-1945

World War I

Between the Franco-Prussian War of 1870-71 and the outbreak of World War I in 1914, railways had been a key factor in several other conflicts. In Africa, the British Royal Engineers had laid lines to Khartoum to support the victorious campaign against the Dervishes of the Sudan and then, in 1899, came the Boer War in South Africa.

The campaigns of this war extended over a vast area, and hundreds of miles separated the ports of the Cape, through which the British forces passed, from the territories where most of the war was fought. To prevent the railways and the military working at cross-purposes, the British established a Department of Military Railways which matched military requirements with actual railway capacity. The lines were almost entirely single-track, and capacity was limited, so it became usual to despatch troops on foot while reserving the trains for their supplies.

In their initial retreat the Boers destroyed much of their railway track, but when they turned to the offensive they rarely restored it; being traditionalists, they preferred horse transport, and even when a railway was available they often made no use of it. They became adept at disablement, however, and on railways close to the war zones the British had to send out parties each dawn to check that Boer commandos had not damaged the track during the night.

Rudimentary armored trains were fitted out, typically consisting of a locomotive in the middle, open cars with armored sides for the infantry, and a flatcar at the head-end with a gun. These were less successful than had been hoped, because they were wrongly regarded as a form of cavalry and sent on incursions into enemy territory. However, unlike cavalry, they had to go back the same way as they had come, which gave opportunities to a wily enemy. It was while riding in an armored train that the young Winston Churchill was captured by the Boers, who had blocked its line of retreat.

Soon after the Boer War came the Russo-Japanese War in 1904, which demonstrated the strategic importance of railways. Although the barely finished Trans-Siberian line was equipped with extra crossing loops and the train service speeded up, the Russians were able to assemble and supply a strong army only in the final months of the campaign, after they had lost the key battles. This was the first major war in which 2-foot gauge transportable railways of the Decauville type were employed. Laid behind the front lines, they were used for bringing up troops and supplies, and for evacuating the wounded.

The big continental military powers depended on railways for their security, which rested on fast mobilization and deployment. For Germany, liable to face a 2-front war against France and Russia, fast mobilization was the basis of the Schlieffen Plan, which envisaged a concentration of troops against France before Russia could mobilize, and then, after France's rapid defeat, a quick railborne redeployment to the east to face the Russians.

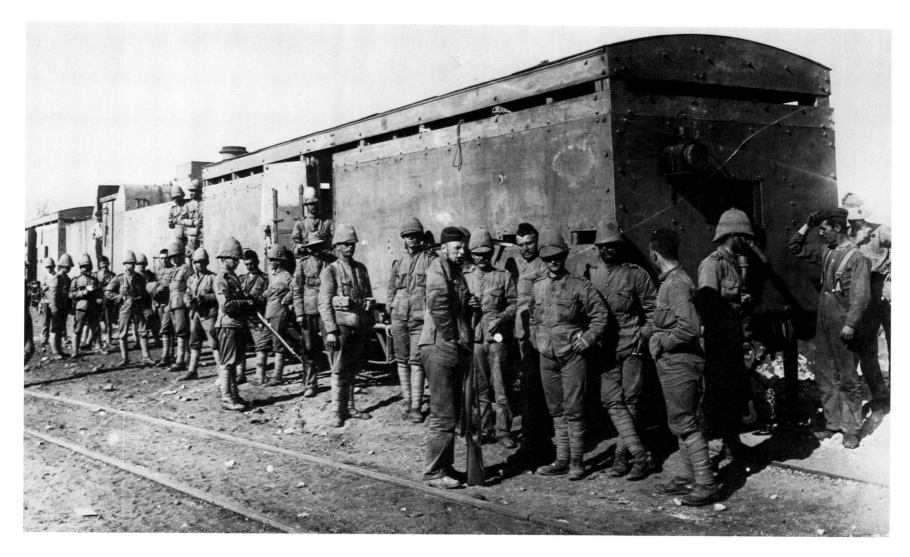

Previous spread: An armored train fitted out by the German army in World War I. Following customary practice, the locomotive was placed in the middle.

Above: A British armored train at Modder River, in the Boer War. The nearest vehicle is for infantry, having been provided with armored sides and firing slits. Armored trains played a small role in this war, and an even smaller role in the 2 world wars, although they were important in the Russian Civil War.

Left: A South African station under the control of British troops during the Boer War period. The rudimentary accommodation provided for the local population should be noted, although British troops also traveled in open freight cars.

Left: August 1914; French residents in Britain return home to join the French army. The picture shows their send-off as they leave Victoria Station, the London terminus of the South Eastern and Chatham Railway.

Below left: A British 6-inch naval gun mounted on a railway chassis for use in the Boer War. This idea enabled heavy guns to be used in the campaign.

Right: War gives a chance for novel ideas to gain acceptance. A few innovations are successful, but most are not. But for the existence of this Boer War photograph, 'Hairy Mary,' the locomotive camouflaged during the siege of Ladysmith, would have been long forgotten.

In peacetime Germany, platforms and paved station areas were built as military loading points and exercises were regularly held to test the readiness of the railways. Railways had a military member on their management councils, and facilities were inspected each year. A mobilization schedule, revised annually, detailed down to the last carrier pigeon the movement of the army and its supplies. There were 2 phases: the mobilization phase in which special trains would take reservists from their home stations to their military depots, and the deployment, in which units would be taken from their depots to allotted places on the frontier.

France, Austria, and Russia had similar, though less detailed, mobilization plans. In the years preceding 1914 the Russians, helped by French advice and money, had been improving their western railways, and also placing their regular army formations nearer the frontier. By that year, the Russian plan could mobilize 66 percent of the immense army in just 3 days longer than the Germans needed to mobilize their whole army. Thus the several weeks difference in deployment times that the Schlieffen Plan relied on could no longer be expected. This was alarming for the German General Staff, which now saw that a victorious war against the Franco-Russian alliance was fast becoming impossible. It was this realization that engendered the 'now or never' spirit among the German military staff in 1914.

Once the war started, the belligerents' mobilization and deployment plans worked faultlessly. Even the bureaucratic, creaking, Austrian administration managed to field its troops in the expected time, while Russia achieved mobilization and deployment several days earlier than planned.

At Cologne, for 2 weeks, 6 westbound military trains per hour rumbled across the key railway bridge over the Rhine. To utilize fully all their railway lines, the German troops had to be spread over a long expanse of frontier. This in turn meant that one arm of the offensive passed through neutral Belgium, with dire diplomatic consequences, while in the south the Duchy of Luxembourg had to be captured for the sake of its key railway junction. A single armored train, sent in as war was declared, did this.

Later, when the German army moved into France, the plans went astray. The offensive outpaced the speed with which the railway battalions could restore and operate the captured French and Belgian railways, with the result that many German formations were reduced to living off the land, which had some effect on their fighting capacity.

In Britain, the transportation of the British Expeditionary Force (BEF) to Southampton was faultless, and as the war progressed the supply of the BEF in France was taken over by the Railway Operating Division of the Royal Engineers, which was composed, for the most part, of soldiers recruited from the home railways. British locomotives and rolling stock were sent to work over the French lines between the Channel ports and the British sector of the front. At Richborough, in Kent, a new port was built to handle train ferries carrying loaded freight cars to France.

Meanwhile, as the war progressed, the British railways were burdened with unprecedented demands. Wisely, the government had set up the Railway Executive Committee (REC) to control the activities of the scores of railway companies; being made up of railway managers, the REC had a good idea of what could and could not be done, and worked very successfully. One consequence was that, because the different railways were co-ordinated and wasteful competition eliminated, they seemed to work far more efficiently than they had in peacetime.

Traffic took new directions. In particular, the poverty-stricken low-traffic Highland Railway was flooded with traffic, for it was the only line serving the Royal Navy's main base at Scapa Flow. The 'Naval Special' ran daily over the more than 700 miles separating London from the northern tip of Scotland. Meanwhile, to enable trains to carry more passengers, restaurant cars were removed from almost all services in Britain. Exhortations to Britons to refrain from traveling for pleasure and holidays, however, were largely unheeded even after a sharp deterrent rise in fares. Railway workshops turned over much of their production to munitions work, with the result that much maintenance was deferred.

For the American railroads, the war really began in 1915, with increased traffic resulting from the flow of supplies ordered by the belligerent powers. Among these supplies were 2-foot gauge locomotives ordered for the field railways of Britain, France, and Russia. The railroads also did well in 1915, with their expeditious southward movement of National Guard units during the Mexican crisis. However, when traffic became heavy, bottlenecks developed, and the companies were in a poor situation to deal with these. Co-ordination was the obvious technical solution, with railroads agreeing to route freight over unusual routes so as to reduce congestion. But the anti-monopoly legislation of the previous decades prohibited this kind of co-operation and, moreover, the companies were unwilling to divert part of their freight over competitors' lines. It was spring 1917 before the railroads felt able and willing to set up their Railroads War Board. This effected some useful changes but with America entering the war, with labor unrest on the railroads, and with the blizzards of late 1917, a traffic crisis developed, and the federal government took over the railroads and set up the United States Railroad Administration (USRA). Then events in the United States closely paralleled what had happened in Britain; the rail network began to work incomparably better. Services were pooled, standard USRA locomotives were built for use on all railroads, competing city ticket offices were closed, and so on. However, on the whole,

this success (and in particular the reasons for it) was not publicized.

When the United States Army landed in France in 1918 it was accompanied by its own railroad service. Soon the United States Transportation Corps was operating trains not only behind the American sector of the front, but also between the Atlantic ports and the Western Front. Most of the American railroad operating troops were professional railroaders and made a good impression, but later reinforcements appear to have been of lower quality. When the war ended the railroad troops were required to stay on for another year and, dispirited, they soon made themselves a nuisance by ignoring French railway instructions and regulations, stopping their trains to make unscheduled calls at station buffets and, it was alleged, molesting travelers.

Above left: A United States Army narrow-gauge locomotive on the Western Front. Hundreds of units of this design were built, and many were sold to the British and Russian war ministries.

Right: Three types of front-line transport and not a wisp of steam in sight. The photograph was taken during a British offensive in August 1917. Internal-combustion engines were ideal for front-line railways, as their exhaust was invisible to enemy artillery observers.

Below: The Durham Light Infantry move up to the Battle of Pilckem Ridge in July 1917.

Postwar Upheaval

World War I marked the end of an age for the railways as well as for society in general, but whereas in western society a brave new world seemed to be dawning, for the railways a brave old world had just disappeared. Gone were the prewar certainties, the knowledge that railways were indispensible, progressive, and profit-making. The war had hastened certain processes and had revealed others, for example the slow decline of profitability, that had been partly hidden before.

To varying degrees, the railways of the belligerents had been worn out. Hardest hit, perhaps, was Belgium, which had been occupied throughout the war. Most of the Belgian locomotives had been evacuated to France; some had even been sent as far as Russia, and by no means all came back. The German railways were run down, and after the war they were administered by the Allies for some years. In Britain, the railways had carried extra traffic during the war and had deferred much maintenance and investment. The government had prevented them raising their rates in line with inflation and, moreover, had forced them to grant wage increases. When the war ended they expected promised compensation payments, but the government refused and only after lengthy argument was a compromise reached.

The American railroads were not released from federal control until 1920, by which time many USRA locomotives had been placed into service. There had been a call for railroad nationalization, since federal control had greatly improved their performance, but the Transportation Act of 1920 simply strengthened the Interstate Commerce Commission (ICC) which from then on was allowed to set minimum as well as maximum railroad rates. The ICC's stated intention of persuading small companies to merge into larger ones had no result.

In Britain there were also calls for nationalization, for the same reasons, but in the end there was a compromise in which the 123 companies were obliged by the 1921 Railways Act to amalgamate into 4 large enterprises. Of the old companies, only the Great Western Railway survived, slightly enlarged by the acquisition of some small Welsh companies. Largest of the new companies was the London Midland and Scottish Railway (LMS), which absorbed, among others, the London and North Western, Midland, and Caledonian railways. Second biggest was the London and North Eastern Railway (LNER), which embraced the Great Northern, Great Eastern, North Eastern, North British and other railways. Smallest of the 'Big Four' was the Southern Railway (SR), serving southern England and distinguished from the others in that most of its revenue came from passengers, rather than freight.

In Germany, where the old state railways had continued even after the proclamation of the German Empire in 1871, there was at last the long-awaited amalgamation into a national network, the Deutsche Reichsbahn (DR), which tended to imitate the practices of its largest constituent, the Prussian State Railways. In France there was already one state railway, the État, which had been formed to take over the burden of several loss-making lines in the west, and in 1938 the remaining mainline railways would be nationalized to form the French National Railways (SNCF).

The French were not alone in having both state and private railways coexisting. In Sweden and Switzerland the process of converting private to state railways has not yet been completed, and probably will not be. In Holland the 2 companies, one private and one state, were not joined into a state company (NS) until 1938. In the new Irish Republic the different railways were amalgamated into the Great Southern Railways which, in 1945, became the nucleus of the state CIE. Private ownership continued in Northern Ireland, until the British railways were themselves nationalized in 1948.

In Canada, when the war ended, there was the profitable and self-confident Canadian Pacific, and some other lines with

Left: An early form of container transport, introduced by the French PLM Railway to carry fruit from southern France to the London markets.

Above right: On the eve of its disappearance as a separate company by incorporation into the new Southern Railway, the SECR tries to attract excursion revenue.

Right: The London and North Eastern Railway keeps up with the modern age in 1924 by attaching a cinema car to the *Flying Scotsman.* This experiment did not last long.

uncertain prospects. These included a state railway, Canadian Government Railways, which had been formed to take over the ailing Intercolonial Railway, the private Grand Trunk, whose main line was a substantially built route from Montreal to Toronto, the Canadian Northern, which was expanding into a coast-to-coast railway, and the Grand Trunk Pacific, which was operating its own main line to the Pacific in the west and also the connecting, government-built, National Transcontinental. Duplication of routes was quite blatant; stretches of the Canadian Pacific and Grand Trunk ran alongside each other between Montreal and Toronto, while the Yellowhead Pass in the Rockies had 2 competing lines laid side-by-side. Government action, or inaction, was largely responsible for this overbuilding, but when the Grand Trunk ran into financial difficulties in 1919, Ottawa refused to help. Its British board of management thereupon voted itself 5 years' salary, and sold the company to the Canadian government. In 1923 the main railways, with the exception of the Canadian Pacific, were amalgamated into a crown corporation, Canadian National Railways which, under the vigorous leadership of its American president, Henry Thornton, became a smart and coherent enterprise.

In South Africa railway nationalization was achieved by a different route. At the end of the Boer War the British Army's Department of Military Railways became the Imperial Military Railways, which took over the captured railways of the Transvaal and Orange Free State. These lines then became the Central South African Railways which in 1910, on the formation of the Union of South Africa, joined with the Cape and the Natal government railways to form a new company; the South African Railways and Harbours.

Australia was different, in that it had a 'national' railway, the federal Commonwealth Railways, coexisting with state railways in most of the states. Full-scale nationalization was not practic-

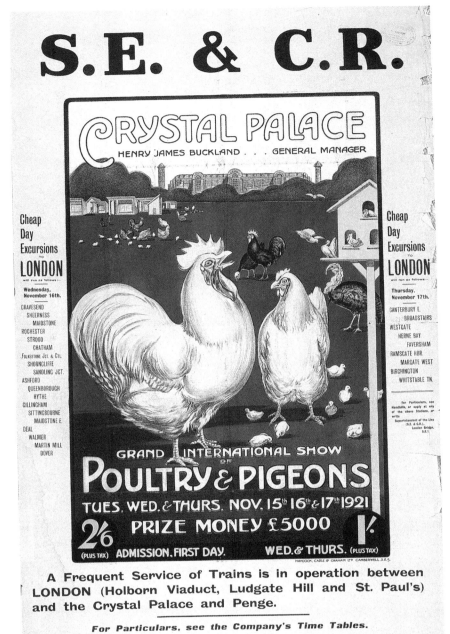

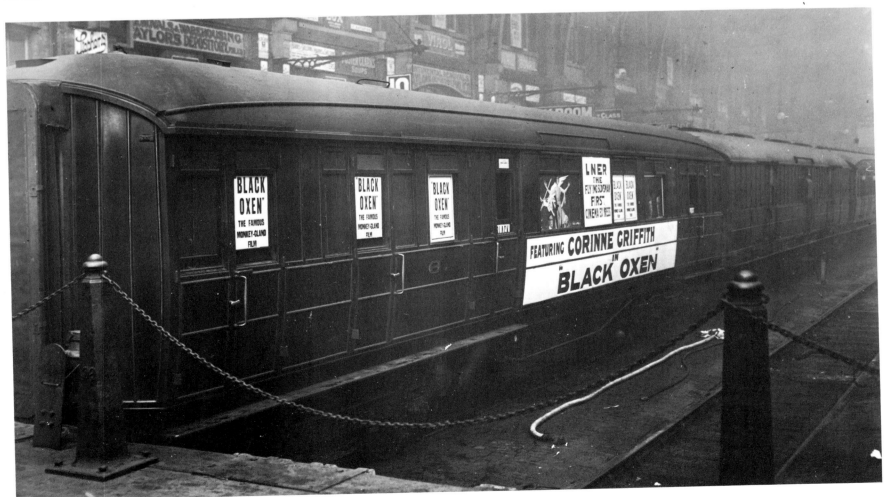

Left: Modernization of passenger-information services at the King's Cross terminus of the London and North Eastern Railway in 1936. The roller train-departure panel lasted for several decades and saved the time of platform staff, who had fewer passenger enquiries to answer. But the timetable display machines were less successful, perhaps because they required too much manipulation.

Above right: Road versus rail in Britain in the 1930s; the LNER (formerly Great Northern Railway) main line, paralleled by the Great North Road.

Right: A remarkable LNER freight train in 1930, on show to combat the new competition from the highway.

able because the state governments were unwilling to hand over their railways to Canberra. Not until political mismanagement had turned the state railways into serious financial burdens did the Australian states consider seriously the idea of handing them to the Commonwealth Railways (now the Australian National Railways). By the mid-1980s the Tasmanian and the main South Australian railways had joined the ANR.

The reorganizations in Europe and Canada probably helped the railways in their struggle against the new competition from road vehicles. World War I had advanced the onset of highway competition by some years (perhaps a decade) for when it ended there were thousands of ex-soldiers who had learned to drive motor trucks, and thousands of army motor trucks for disposal at knockdown prices. The consequence was a multiplication of small-scale, often one-man and one-truck, highway companies,

some of which developed into large trucking companies that began to skim away the railways' traffic. Specializing at first in the most highly rated traffic, like manufactured goods, highway operators could deliver door-to-door, offer cheaper rates and, because trucks did not need to wait in yards for a train to be assembled, a faster service. The railways retaliated in several ways. In particular, they agitated at the political level for fair treatment, by which they meant that highway operators did not pay for, or repair, the roads they used and were not obliged to carry any traffic that was offered, as the railways were. In continental Europe this political effort had some success; governments realized that if railways lost their high-rated traffic they might be unable to operate low-traffic lines or carry their bulk traffic so cheaply. In Britain, where the highway lobby was, and remained, strong, the railways' pleas were less successful.

Short of political help, the only recourse was to compete on price and service, and this the railways of Britain and the United States tried to do. Fast freight trains and more specialized freight cars were among their expedients, as were efforts to cut down costs so as to give scope for rate reductions. In some ways the competition, therefore, benefitted the railways, for it obliged them to do things that they had previously neglected. Cost accounting, for example, had hitherto languished in a prehistoric

condition both in the United States and Britain, with railway companies quite ignorant of how much it cost to carry various categories of freight.

The coming of the internal combustion engine was only one advance of the time which helped to rob the railways of their reputation as technological pacemakers. Suddenly, the railways seemed old-fashioned and not so essential after all. In conscious and unconscious reaction to this feeling, managements began to

Right: A celebrated and often imitated poster of the Southern Railway.

Left: To improve public relations, the new British companies periodically staged exhibitions of the latest rolling stock. Here the LNER *Flying Scotsman* locomotive is among the exhibits.

seek ways of altering the public image of their activities. The streamlined passenger train was perhaps the most blatant effort to recapture a spirit of modernity, but there were others too. Progressive artists were hired to design posters and advertising calendars. A few railways used such artists to design a whole house-style for train liveries, station signs, maps and all other railway features susceptible of redesign. The Southern Railway in Britain introduced a malachite green livery and began to reconstruct its stations in the modern idiom, with extended use of concrete and other up-to-date materials. In the United States, although many companies still preferred to build ponderous, monolithic railroad stations, there were others which were more ambitious, hiring architects to build stations with a hint of the futuristic about them. Cincinnati Union Terminal was perhaps the best-known, but not the only one, of these extremely up-to-date stations.

The Streamliners

The first streamlined train, the *Windsplitter*, appeared in the United States as early as 1900. On trial over the Baltimore and Ohio Railroad, it averaged 87mph for several miles, but greater speeds had been hoped for, and the project was abandoned. Paradoxically it failed because, as with the later streamliners, its sole purpose was to reduce wind resistance. This was a very unrealistic aim, and streamlining when it finally blossomed in the 1930s justified itself in terms not of wind resistance, but of publicity.

Wind pressure can require vastly increased horsepower to overcome it, but this arises not from head winds but from side winds, which push the train against the leeward rail, causing the wheel flanges to grind heavily. There is little a designer can do to reduce this, except strive to present a train with clean, smooth, sides. Head-on resistance is negligible up to about 70mph, and even above that figure it builds up slowly. No doubt the 126mph speed record won by the streamlined British locomotive *Mallard* would not have been achieved in the absence of streamlining, but at that speed streamlining probably only accounted for about 5mph. The *Windsplitter* seemed to recognize this, for it was the train, rather than the locomotive that was streamlined. But the rolling stock was heavy, and speeds above 90mph were not met.

The first of the later generation of streamliners were self-propelled, rather than locomotive-hauled, trains. In 1933 the Budd Company built a 2-car, vaguely streamlined, train for the Texas and Pacific Railroad, but the main public interest in this was focused on the French-designed Michelin pneumatic tires. In France, modernistic rail cars incorporating racing-car technology and designed by Bugatti were attracting attention, and it would not be long before the GWR in Britain would introduce single-unit streamlined diesel rail cars.

The first 2 examples of the long-distance, mainline, streamlined train appeared in the United States almost simultaneously in 1934. Both were 3-car and articulated (that is, adjoining car ends shared the support of a single truck). The streamlining was only one of their advanced features. Others included the power units, which were 600hp internal combustion engines. The first to appear was the Union Pacific's M-10000, built of aluminum alloy by Pullman Standard and powered by a distillate engine. It

Above: The Union Pacific Railroad exhibits its new streamliners. On the right is M-10003, the 1936 *City of Denver* train, and on the left is a General Motors diesel-electric unit, part of the 1937 *City of San Francisco* train, jointly operated by the Union Pacific, Southern Pacific, and Chicago and North Western railroads.

Left: The *Coronation Scot* of the LMS, hauled by Pacific locomotive *Queen Elizabeth*, tackling one of the long gradients encountered in the northern part of its run.

was followed some months later by the somewhat larger M-10001, which was diesel powered. Meanwhile, the Burlington Railroad had introduced its *Zephyr*, similar in concept but powered by electric motors supplied from a generator driven by a General Motors diesel engine. This was the first of the streamliners to enter regular service, plying between Lincoln, Nebraska, and Kansas City. The 2 Union Pacific streamliners toured much of the United States, breaking speed records now and again to retain public attention, and then went into regular service, with M-10000 running between Kansas City and Salina, a short run, and M-10001 becoming the *City of Portland*, and running between Chicago and Portland in less than 40 hours.

As a publicity enterprise, the streamliners were wildly successful. They were associated in the public mind with speed (for 60mph schedules were typical) and with modernity. Civil airliners at this time were only just becoming metal monoplanes and their radial engines were far from streamlined, so in terms of sleekness the train was outmatching the airliner, and in some ways resembled the racing car. Soon, most big railroads were introducing streamlined trains. The first non-articulated streamliners, the 'Rebels' of the Gulf, Mobile and Northern, were built by the American Car and Foundry in 1935. Placed in the St Louis to New Orleans service, they were the first streamliners in the South and also the first to carry train hostesses.

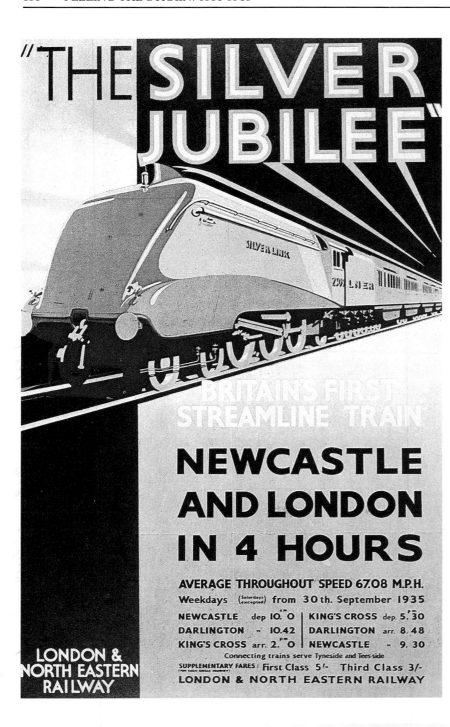

"THE SILVER JUBILEE"

BRITAINS FIRST STREAMLINE TRAIN

NEWCASTLE AND LONDON IN 4 HOURS

AVERAGE THROUGHOUT SPEED 67.08 M.P.H.

Weekdays (Saturdays excepted) from 30th. September 1935

NEWCASTLE	dep 10. 0	KING'S CROSS	dep 5. 30
DARLINGTON	– 10.42	DARLINGTON	arr. 8. 48
KING'S CROSS	arr. 2. 0	NEWCASTLE	– 9. 30

Connecting trains serve Tyneside and Tees-side

SUPPLEMENTARY FARES (FOR EACH SINGLE JOURNEY): First Class 5/-   Third Class 3/-

LONDON & NORTH EASTERN RAILWAY

LONDON & NORTH EASTERN RAILWAY

Left: Modern art accompanies modern trains; a poster advertising the LNER *Silver Jubilee* streamliner.

Below: The streamline age even touched the railways of troubled Spain. The Talgo train, of which a late example is shown here, was low slung and supported on single-axle wheelsets; it was capable of moderately high speeds on Spain's winding railways and was given a streamlined finish, more for show than speed.

Right: Dominion of New Zealand, one of the LNER 'A4'-type locomotives, specially painted to match the 2-tone blue *Coronation* train.

Many of the new streamliners were steam-hauled, the typical low-cost expedient being the clothing of existing locomotives in an outer skin which, all too often, resembled nothing more speedy than an upturned bathtub. Even cheaper was the bullet nose, preferred by several economy-minded managements (including, after World War II, the Indian Railways, which operated no really fast trains but ordered hundreds of the fast-looking 'WP' Class Pacific locomotives).

To provide reserves, there were many more streamlined locomotives than streamlined trains, and the surplus engines were used to haul non-streamlined trains, giving passengers the useful impression that they were traveling in a streamliner. Some railways built streamlined locomotives but not streamlined trains. Among them were the Canadian National and its American subsidiary the Grand Trunk Western, which employed 10 streamlined 4-8-4 locomotives between Montreal and Chicago. In Australia, the Victorian Railways had some streamlined Pacifics for use on the *Spirit of Progress* Sydney to Melbourne interstate express, while the New South Wales Government Railways streamlined the first 5 of its war-built '38' Class Pacifics. But it

was the post-World War II French National Railways which used the image-building idea to ridiculous excess, when they took some superannuated 4-6-0 locomotives, embellished them with bullet noses and smoke deflectors which were not far removed from angels' wings, and placed them at the head of crack trains, the 'Trains Drapeaux', between Paris and eastern France.

It was in Britain that the streamlined steam train attained its greatest sophistication. The London and North Eastern Railway, aware of the successful German high-speed diesel *Flying Hamburger* train, envisaged a similar train. However, on the advice of its chief mechanical engineer, Nigel Gresley, it decided to introduce a steam streamliner instead. The result was the *Silver Jubilee* London to Newcastle service introduced in 1935, hauled by a new class of streamlined Pacific locomotives. On a trial run, this train ran 43 miles at an average of 100mph. In 1937 came the *Coronation*, hauled by the same locomotives and providing a high-speed London to Edinburgh service over the East-Coast route. Meanwhile, the LMS Railway responded on the West-Coast route with the *Coronation Scot*, also hauled by streamlined Pacifics, which reached 114mph on trial.

Above left: The *Flying Scotsman*
leaves King's Cross in London,
hauled, on this rare occasion, by an
experimental and ultimately
unsuccessful high-pressure
locomotive.

Above right: One of 5 streamlined
4-8-4 locomotives used inside
Canada by the Canadian National
Railways for its Montreal to Chicago
trains. Its United States subsidiary,
the Grand Trunk Western, owned 5
others.

Right: The Union Pacific Railroad's
City of Salina, the first streamlined
train.

Train Services

Although the streamliners attracted public attention, they were only a small minority of trains. For the average railway client what was important was the general level of service. The inter-war period was a time when the customer was beginning to see that the railway was rarely the only option. Highway operators were offering a good cheap service for many commodities and while passengers might rarely fly, many could elect to buy a car, or if too poor to do either of these, could still travel on the inter-city bus, less comfortable, but cheaper than the train.

Partly because of this competition, partly because the radical improvement brought by the streamliners filtered down to other, lesser services, and partly because there were technical advances, railway passenger and freight train services did improve quite significantly in the inter-war years.

Average train speeds increased. The speed records that were periodically broken were not in themselves helpful to passengers, but they showed that the locomotives, trains and tracks were capable of higher speeds than before World War I. By the early 1930s, the world's fastest regularly scheduled train was reckoned to be the *Cheltenham Flyer* of the GWR in Britain, which in 1932 was accelerated to an average of 71.4mph over the 77 miles from Swindon to London. Later, the LNER's *Coronation*, by covering the 188 miles from London to York in 157 minutes, slightly surpassed this average. By then, the United States streamliners were in service with, for example, the Milwaukee Railroad's steam *Hiawatha* which regularly exceeded 100mph and the Burlington's diesel *Denver Zephyr* which, on one occasion, covered the 1017 miles from Denver to Chicago at an average speed of 83mph.

Elsewhere in North America there had been occasional regressions, usually taking the form of slowing down trains that had been over-accelerated in the heat of competition. The competition between both the New York Central and Pennsylvania rail-roads for the New York to Chicago overnight Pullman traffic had resulted in both the *Twentieth Century Limited* and the *Broadway Limited* offering 18-hour schedules between the 2 cities. In the 1920s the schedules were of 20 hours, the 2 companies having chosen to compete in terms of service and advertising, rather than speed. In Canada, the Canadian Pacific and Canadian National did something which the anti-trust laws prevented United States railroads from doing; they actually colluded with each other to dampen competition. In the early 1920s the 2 companies had competed strongly on the trunk Montreal to Toronto route, where the single-track CP paralleled the double-track CN. The CP, in an unsuccessful effort to match the CN's 6-hour timing for the 335 miles, did manage to schedule a train over 124 miles of the course at an average speed of 68mph, which was a world record at the time for a regularly scheduled train, but soon afterward the 2 companies agreed to run 'pool trains.' These were jointly operated, each company providing a share of the locomotives and cars. The Ottawa to Toronto service was included and later the Montreal to Quebec route.

Many railway managements, aware that the automobile and the aircraft could not compete in terms of space per passenger, introduced or renovated luxury trains of moderate speed in which the journey could be regarded as a holiday, rather than a necessity. Many of the Pullman trains circulating over the United States railroads alongside the more glamorous streamliners, came into this category, especially the long transcontinental trains with their observation cars and sophisticated dining-car menus. This tradition was also alive in Europe, where the pre-1914 international sleeping-car trains like the *Orient Express* and *Nord Express* had set high standards for supplementary-fare passengers. New trains were introduced in Europe, often providing accommodation for the less wealthy. Among them was the *Golden Arrow*, introduced in the 1920s between London and

Left: An Italian freight car, having crossed the English Channel by train-ferry, delivers its cargo of cheese in a London freight terminal.

Above right: Apart from the load, which is girders for a new bridge, there is nothing distinctive about this LNER publicity shot of the late 1920s. British railways' inter-war freight operations were still essentially of the nineteenth century.

Right: The *Cheltenham Flyer*, proudly announcing its status as the world's fastest train, speeds toward London in 1931, on a new record-breaking run.

Left: One of the daily fast-freight trains, operated by the LNER in the 1930s. The locomotive is a mixed-traffic 2-6-0 type, designed for fast freights and ordinary passenger trains. Two of the small containers used by the British railways can be seen just behind the locomotive.

Right: The Southern Pacific Railroad makes its bid for the bulk wine traffic from California to the eastern states.

Paris. It was a day service, and was unusual in that it provided Pullman rather than Wagons-Lits vehicles. It really consisted of 2 trains, one on the British and one on the French side, with a steamer connection across the English Channel. Another introduction was the *Train Bleu*, providing an opulently luxurious service from Calais and Paris down to the French Riviera. In the mid-1930s the *Night Ferry* was introduced. This was a Wagons-Lits sleeper train which joined London with Paris and Brussels, with the train making an overnight Channel crossing aboard a train ferry.

What was perhaps the most luxurious of the inter-war trains was the *Blue Train* of the South African Railways. This magnificently equipped train was introduced in 1939 and provided a dust-proofed, air-conditioned environment for its lucky passengers; lucky, because not only was a high price payable for using this train, but also because places were strictly limited — to provide space for the various on-board services, barely 100 passengers were carried and reservations had to be made long in advance. This train covered the 999 miles from Cape Town to Pretoria in 27 hours; it was not an especially fast train, but that schedule compared favorably with the 44 hours needed by the fastest train on this route in 1910.

In Australia the late 1930s witnessed the introduction of 2 notable luxury trains. The *Spirit of Progress* was brought in by the Victorian Railways in 1937, and ran from Melbourne to Albury, where it connected with the New South Wales Government Railways' *Sydney Express*. It was very much in the style of the American streamliner, with its cars air-smoothed and made of lightweight alloy. It was usually a train of 12 vehicles, and was scheduled at an average of 53mph. Meanwhile, Commonwealth Railways was operating a transcontinental service between Port Pirie and Kalgoorlie at an average speed of 28mph. The train provided first-class sleepers with 20 passengers per car and second-class with 36. Its parlor car had a piano and the first-class passengers could take a shower. As on an ocean liner, which it somewhat resembled, the fare included the price of meals.

In most countries there were creditable efforts to improve the speed and comfort of trains on secondary routes. Two interesting solutions to the problem of high speed over curving track appeared during this period. The Canadian Pacific designed and built some locomotives of the unusual 4-4-4 wheel arrangement, providing high power output with a minimum rigid wheelbase, and in Spain, the 'Talgo' train appeared. The latter was a light-weight train with a low center of gravity, with one axle per vehicle; the non-axled end of each car resting on the axled end of the next. This solution was very successful in Spain, but less so in the United States, where it was tried in the 1950s.

Although it was their passenger services that were most in the public eye, the majority of railway owners were more concerned about their competitive position against truck operators. To meet the competition, the fast-freight train was the favorite weapon. The first American fast overnight freight was the 1931 *Blue Streak* of the Cotton Belt Railroad, which was soon imitated by other railroads. Many of these ran at passenger train speeds, and some had specially painted cars. Technically, the United States railroads were better equipped than the British to operate fast, or 'hot-shot,' freights. The automatic 'buck-eye' coupler had been imposed on all American railroads by federal law as early as 1893. Apart from speeding up train formation and saving the life and limb of yard-men, it also enabled higher outputs to be transmitted down the train without fear of broken couplings. Moreover, in North America, the automatic brake was added to freight cars. The situation was different in Britain where the crude, loose, hook-and-link coupling was still fitted to most freight cars, which on the whole, were lacking automatic brakes. The British railways' solution was to classify freight trains in accordance to the proportion of cars fitted with continuous brakes and screw couplings, ranging from Class '1' (all vehicles with automatic brakes) to Class '9' (slow freights with hand-brakes only). Class '1' freights were introduced between the important traffic centers in Britain and were fast enough to offer delivery of consignments the next morning. Fortunately, British railways relied for most of their freight revenue on the bulk consignments for which rail transport was so suitable: coal, ores, timber and building materials. These were carried at low rates and did not face highway competition. At the same time, however, the practice of maintaining freight stations every few miles along the tracks meant that there was much small-scale peddling of individual, often half-loaded, freight cars by regular pickup freight trains, which was a high-cost, low-revenue operation.

Steam Locomotive Development

In the United States, locomotive design was dominated by William Woodard's 'Superpower' designs, built by the Lima Locomotive Works. Facing competition, the American railroads required higher horsepower so as to offer faster schedules without reducing train size. Woodard solved this problem by incorporating a 4-wheel trailing truck, which allowed very big fireboxes to be used. His first venture was what was virtually a 2-8-2 built as a 2-8-4, and many 2-8-4s or 'Berkshires' were subsequently built for the railroads. His 2-10-4 for heavy freight, 4-6-4 for fast passenger traffic, and finally the 4-8-4, or 'Northern,' for heavy mixed traffic, followed. Apart from the large firebox, served by mechanical stokers, which became commonplace in North America between the wars, Woodard introduced other improvements, including a jointed connecting rod.

Alongside the 'Superpower' engines, the Mallet type of articulated locomotive continued to thrive. The Union Pacific improved its front suspension in the 'Challenger' class, enabling it to handle quite fast trains, including passenger trains on occasion. It was a development of the 'Challengers,' the Union Pacific's 'Big Boy' 4-8-8-4, that remained the world's biggest steam locomotives, weighing almost 600 tons in working order with tender, and able to handle 3600-ton trains. These machines were a compelling illustration of the wide divergence between American and British and European practice. Rugged, huge, tolerant of poor maintenance, they were designed for hauling very heavy loads with best possible reliability. In Europe, on the other hand, the accent at this time was on fuel economy, high performance in terms of power/weight ratios, and an acceptance of features demanding careful and frequent maintenance.

In Britain, the blend of American, British and continental practice that had resulted in a superb range of locomotives for the GWR had its culmination after World War I. The GWR continued with 4-6-0 designs, enlarging them to produce the outstanding 'Castle' and 'King' passenger locomotives, and introducing a good mixed-traffic locomotive with the 'Halls.' The inter-war years were, perhaps, most noteworthy for the proliferation of mixed-traffic designs, the idea being that a locomotive with driving wheel diameters halfway between the 4 feet 7 inches of typical freight locomotives and the 6 feet 8 inches of fast passenger locomotives would be capable of hauling all trains except the very heaviest freights and the very fastest passenger trains. Such locomotives would consequently spend more hours in traffic, and so produce economies. The idea had arisen earlier; indeed, the American 4-4-0 in the nineteenth century was long regarded as a dual-purpose engine, but it was only in the cost-conscious 1920s and 1930s that the mixed-traffic locomotive became widespread in Britain.

Unlike the GWR, the LNER and LMS preferred Pacific locomotives for their faster passenger trains. The LNER adopted the type designed by Nigel Gresley, of which *Flying Scotsman* became the most famous unit. Improved, and with streamlining, this 3-cylinder design developed into the 'Silver Jubilees,' one of which, *Mallard*, won the authenticated world speed record for steam traction at slightly over 126mph. Gresley was an innovative designer, and introduced wheel arrangements which were quite novel in Britain. For mixed traffic, his 'Green Arrows' had the 2-6-2 arrangement, and he also designed a 2-8-2, the *Cock o' the North* for heavy passenger service. The latter was not very successful and was rebuilt by Gresley's successor, Edward Thompson, who reverted to the 4-6-0 arrangement for his own mixed-traffic class, the handsome but unremarkable 'B1' type.

The LMS was plagued by animosity and acrimony between the managers and engineers who had come to it from the constituent

Above: Grand Trunk Western Railroad locomotives at Detroit. These are representative of the 2 most common wheel arrangements for heavy United States locomotives of the inter-war period. No 6330, leaving on the left with a passenger train, is a 'Northern' (4-8-4), and the other locomotive is a 'Mikado,' or 2-8-2.

Right: Drysllwyn Castle, one of the Great Western Railway's celebrated 'Castle' class passenger locomotives, enjoying a second life as a preserved but working exhibit.

companies. When former Midland Railway men took charge of locomotive policy, they seemed more interested in scrapping L & NW Railway designs than in producing plans for new locomotives. For a much-needed heavy-passenger locomotive the LMS, unusually, turned to a private locomotive builder for the *Royal Scot* 4-6-0. Finally, in the early 1930s, William Stanier, a GWR man, was appointed chief mechanical engineer and produced a range of successful types that first incorporated, and then improved upon, GWR design features. For heavy passenger work he introduced the 'Princess Elizabeths,' and then the 'Duchesses,' both 4-6-2s. Some of the latter were streamlined and one of them, *Duchess of Abercorn*, produced 3300 indicated horsepower on test; a quite remarkable output for a locomotive of that size. Among Stanier's other successes were his Class '5' mixed-traffic 4-6-0 and Class '8' freight 2-8-0, which both lasted up to the end of steam.

The fourth and smallest of the British companies, the SR, was being electrified, and steam locomotive requirements were rather small. In the first 2 decades, many 2-6-0 mixed-traffic units

were built, and a handful of 4-6-0s of the 'King Arthur' and 'Lord Nelson' types. But in the 1940s, despite the war, a new chief mechanical engineer, Oliver Bulleid, produced 2 startling designs. His 'Q1' 0-6-0 was a remarkably ugly machine, designed with a view to saving metal, while his Pacifics, the 'Merchant Navys' and the more numerous but smaller 'West Countrys,' were extremely innovative. They were enveloped in a smooth shroud to reduce air resistance, their 3 cylinders were controlled by a valve gear operated by chains and working in an oil bath, and they had American-style disc driving wheels. Many of them were rebuilt as less complex locomotives after the war.

In Germany, the new unified railway, DR, followed the Prussian locomotive tradition; priority was given to simplicity and reliability, producing locomotives that had a lower power/weight ratio than those of other countries, but which were well liked by the men who had to operate them. The outstanding design was the 2-10-0 that became the basis for the *Kriegslok*, built by the thousand and used in most parts of German-occupied Europe during World War II.

Above left: A publicity line-up of the Great Western's most powerful locomotives, the 'King' class.

Above right: A 'Schools' class train of the Southern Railway at Waterloo Station, London, in 1937. Reversion to the nineteenth century 4-4-0 wheel arrangement for these modern engines was unusual, but they became a very successful class.

Right: An inter-war 4-8-2 of the South African Railways. This class, having a light axle-weight, was used on many secondary lines.

But it was in France that the most exciting developments took place. Here André Chapelon introduced, or reintroduced, so many perfections that his rebuildings of certain existing locomotives could almost double their power outputs while hardly changing their weight. He was a protagonist of compounding, but that was not the secret of his success. He widened and smoothed internal steam passages to conserve energy, he incorporated feedwater heating, higher temperature superheating, and he improved drafting. His 'Kylchap' exhaust, usually including a double chimney (that is, with 2 orifices) provided a draft that was strong and smooth, powerful enough to draw ample air through the fire, but not powerful enough to drag coal particles with it. This Kylchap exhaust was fitted to some British locomotives, including the very successful rebuilt version of the 'Royal Scots.' Chapelon's mixed-traffic '141P' 2-8-2 was probably the world's most successful design in terms of the power/weight ratio.

Right: No 2929 of the Canadian Pacific Railway, with the unusual wheel arrangement of 4-4-4, leaves Montreal.

Below: One of the celebrated 4-8-4 locomotives, used to haul the *Daylight* trains of the Southern Pacific Railroad. On the right is an example of the 'cab-in-front' Mallet freight locomotives, used by this railroad on lines where, in tunnels, locomotive men were in danger of being asphyxiated by the exhaust.

Unorthodox Steam Power

The requirement for ever more horsepower within the existing limits of axle weight, wheelbase, and width, meant that many engineers began to seek radical alternatives to the conventional steam locomotive. The Mallet and Garratt had themselves been radical solutions in their time, but they were both approaching the limits of their development and, moreover, perpetuated the inherent economic weakness of the steam locomotive; its inability to convert more than about 6 to 10 percent of coal's potential energy into tractive work.

Steam turbine locomotives received a good deal of attention for, in theory, they promised better thermal efficiency and, because of their smooth operation, less 'hammerblow' on the track. But for maximum efficiency they needed a condenser to convert used steam into warm feedwater, and for reverse working they needed either complex gearing or a second turbine. In Britain the Ramsay-Macleod turbine locomotive of 1924, of the 4-4-0+0-4-4 wheel arrangement was fairly successful but its power/weight ratio was too low to make it worthwhile. On the LMS Railway, the 'Turbomotive' 4-6-2 had parts in common with the 'Princess Elizabeth' class of conventional locomotives. It had a small reverse turbine, and the main turbine produced 2600hp. It worked quite well from 1935 to 1951, but being a single and special unit, when it needed repairs these tended to take a long time, so its utilization rate was low. In the United States, the Pennsylvania Railroad's Class 'S2' 6-8-6 turbomotive suffered from the same problem. It was technically successful, but

because of time spent out of service could not compete with diesels. The Swedish Ljungstrom turbine locomotives were the most successful. These had a single turbine driving through gearing and had a remarkably low water consumption. One sent to Britain worked reasonably well but was soon withdrawn, while several others worked for a long time and successfully in Sweden.

Steam-electric locomotives used steam to generate electricity, which was then fed to electric traction motors. This idea emerged as early as 1890, with the Heilmann locomotive of the French Western Railway. The later British Reid-Ramsay locomotives were similar, but had condensers. They worked satisfactorily, but the power/weight ratio was low. On the eve of World War II the UP in the United States was trying 2 steam-electrics with very high boiler pressure and watertube boilers; they seemed promising but the war put an end to their trials. After World War II the Chesapeake and Ohio (C & O) and the Norfolk and Western (N & W) railroads, both of which were in close contact with the coal industry, tried steam-turbine-electrics as alternatives to diesel traction. The 3 built for the C & O in 1947-48 were unsuccessful, but No 2300 of the N & W lasted longer. This locomotive, at 586 tons, the world's biggest single-unit locomotive, had a watertube boiler and 12 powered axles.

Attempts to combine the flexibility of the steam locomotive with the thermal efficiency of the diesel were uniformly unsuccessful. The British Kitson-Still of 1927 had 8 opposed cylinders

Left: A Franco-Crosti locomotive of the Italian State Railways. The drums, through which the hot exhaust gases passed to heat the feedwater, can be clearly seen, as can one of the unprepossessing chimneys.

Right: An experimental French streamlined locomotive. Like the German streamliners, this prototype was never developed. Many engineers, probably rightly, believed that streamlining had more to do with fashion than with efficiency.

Left: A condensing 4-8-4 of the South African Railways.

Below: The Pennsylvania Railroad's 4-4-4-4 of the 1940s. These locomotives, used in passenger service, were virtually multi-cylinder 4-8-4s with divided drive.

Right: A steam-electric locomotive tried by the Union Pacific Railroad on the eve of World War II.

Below right: An unsuccessful attempt at a high-pressure locomotive. This LNER project also had a marine-type watertube boiler.

which worked on a 4-stroke diesel cycle, aided by steam acting on the passive side of their pistons when extra power was needed. In the 1930s and 1940s the Soviet Railways expended much effort on their 'Teploparovozy.' These had conventional boilers which supplied steam to cylinders that had opposed pistons. When a sufficiently high speed was reached, the central parts of the cylinders were switched from steam to diesel combustion, so that steam propelled the pistons on their inward stroke, and diesel combustion on their outward stroke. Unlike many other more hopeful innovations, these follies received ample financial support, but after 10 years of glowing reports they were acknowledged to be failures; the basic problem of equalizing the thrust of the diesel and steam impulses was never solved satisfactorily.

High-pressure steam locomotives, which used steam not at the conventionally low 150-300 psi railway pressure but at 400-1000 psi, and thereby increased both power and fuel economy, were tried by several railways, especially in Germany. They included the *Fury*, an LMS 4-6-0 which suffered a fatal steam burst, No 10000 of the LNER, which was a compound with watertube boiler, *L F Loree* of the Delaware and Hudson Railroad, and No 5905 of the Canadian Pacific.

Condenser locomotives for use in arid regions had some success. Henschel of Germany specialized in these, and their designs were adopted by Soviet Railways for mass production of a 2-10-0 type for use in the Central Asian deserts. The same scheme was used for the massive '25' Class of 4-8-4 for the South African Railways. In World War II the Russian design was

A NEW STEAM-ELECTRIC RAILWAY GIANT

NEARLY two years have been spent by American engineers in designing this new 5,000 h.p. steam-electric locomotive which has just been completed for the Union Pacific Railroad. It is a distinctly new type of motive power on wheels, in fact it is an electric locomotive carrying its own power plant. Steam is generated in a patent oil-fired boiler to the terrific pressure of 1,500 lbs. per sq. in. at a temperature of 920° F. This steam passes to a superheater and then to the turbines. These turbines (of high and low pressure) are used to drive the main generator through reduction gearing of approximately 10 to 1. This generator supplies current direct to the six traction motors situated on each side of the six pairs of driving wheels. This is the motive power. A 220 volt alternating generator is also coupled to the same shaft as the main generator and supplies current for train air-conditioning, traction motor ventilators and other accessories.

Water is required from time to time to compensate for losses due to evaporation, etc., and this water is carried in tanks on either side of the nose of the locomotive, in front of the cab. An auxiliary turbine set is used to drive the fuel-oil pumps, boiler draught fans, compressors and the condenser fans. This locomotive is to haul the express trains between Chicago and the Pacific Coast, and is capable of 120 m.p.h.

KEY TO NUMBERS ABOVE AND PLAN ON LEFT

1. Door to concealed coupler
2. Door between water tanks to cabin
3. Searchlight
4. Harker light
5. Water tank
6. Electric windscreen wiper
7-7A. Sirens
8. Vertical light for warning at level crossings
9. Dual control cabin
9A. Driver (on plan only)
10. Exciter for main generator
11. 220-volt alternator for train air-conditioning, etc.
12. Main generator supplying current to the six traction motors
13. Ventilating trunk
14. Gear case
15. High-pressure turbine
16. Low-pressure turbine
17. Train heating evaporator
18. Exhaust steam pipe to condensers
19. Superheated steam pipe to turbines
20. Special oil-fired boiler
21. Superheater
21A. Boiler draught fan (on plan only)
21B. Auxiliary turbine set (on plan only)
22. Exhaust feeder pipe
23. Driving shaft for fans
24. Fans for drawing air through the sides of the condensers and discharging through the roof
25. Condensers for converting used steam back to distilled water
26. Oil fuel tanks
27. Outside louvres for condensers
28. Rear bogie truck
29. Rear driving wheels
30. Main control contactors
31. Front driving wheels
32. Brake cylinders
33. One of the six traction motors driving each driving wheel axle
34. Front bogie truck
35. Brake cylinder

Turbine set with casing removed to show blades and 10 to 1 reduction gearing. The high-pressure turbine is the further one and the low pressure in the foreground. The main generator is on the right.

'copied back' to provide the German forces in Russia with their own condenser locomotives.

The Franco-Crosti and Crosti locomotives were also quite successful. In these the exhaust steam passed through 1 or 2 drums to heat the boiler feedwater. This did bring a fuel economy, but also higher maintenance costs, so it was only in Italy, where coal was expensive, that these locomotives were used extensively, although the postwar British Railways experimented with them.

The Pennsylvania Railroad adopted the duplex drive locomotive (first used on the B & O Railroad in 1937) and its 52 4-4-4-4 locomotives became the basic steam passenger type in the years before the introduction of diesel power. These distinctive locomotives, which resembled non-articulated Mallets, were vir-

tually 4-8-4s in which the 4 driving axles were split into two 2-axle units, each powered by its own outside cylinders. This layout lessened the track stresses experienced by heavy locomotives traveling at high speed.

Among other innovations, one which proved exceptionally useless was the 4-14-4 designed by Soviet engineering students in the 1930s and foisted onto an unenthusiastic Soviet Railways management. There were 14 driving axles in a rigid frame which was a world record, for good reasons, as with that length of wheelbase the locomotive was only safe on straight track. An even stranger prototype was the 3-unit, 4-boiler, 0-6-2+2-4-2+0-4-2+2-6-0. This was designed by an Italian but built and tried in Belgium.

Above: A Sentinel yard locomotive, one of a type used at several British locations. It had a small high-pressure boiler and chain drive.

Left: A fireless steam locomotive. Such units, charged periodically by a stationary boiler, were used at locations where sparks could be dangerous.

Right: American- and British-design Pacifics in India. The 'WP' type, on the left, was designed in the United States, but was built in many countries for India during the 1950s. The 'Xa' type, on the right, was built in Britain before World War II.

The Locomotive Exported

In the early days of railways, companies would buy the locomotives that happened to be on offer by the builders. Thus the Stephenson 'Patentee' type could be seen at work in several countries. As new locomotive works were opened, different schools of locomotive design became evident. The divergence of American practice came quite early, the bar-framed, haystack-firebox imports from Edward Bury being the starting point and when locomotive works were opened in France, Germany and Belgium, railway engines began to assume national characteristics.

Sometimes the divergences were fundamental, but sometimes only superficial, being marked by preferred designs of components, such as chimneys and cabs. Within a given country, too, individual railways might develop their own sub-style of locomotive. This was particularly the case when a company had its own locomotive works. In Britain most railways built their own locomotives, which could usually be distinguished from those of other companies by their details and style. In America a few railroads built their own. Among these were the Pennsylvania and Canadian Pacific railroads, both of which developed a very distinctive corporate style for their locomotives.

In the twentieth century the French locomotive was very distinctive, not only because of the wide use of compounding but because of the somewhat refined design of components. French engine-men were the best trained in the world, and they were entrusted with locomotives that American railroads would have found impossibly delicate. In Austria, the tradition established by Karl Gölsdorf was unique. Faced with the need to provide high power and low axle weights, this designer built engines with very light frames and boilers which were sharply tapered to save weight at the front end and were designed for low pressures so that thin plates could be used. He also omitted running plates and splashers to save weight. Such gaunt, but effective, engines were not seen outside central Europe.

When locomotive builders exported their products they were, in effect, exporting their style and their technology. Thus it was not surprising that French-style locomotives should appear in Spain, North Africa, and Indo-China. In different British colonies, locomotives of identical types could be encountered. The German style of locomotive spread to the Russian Empire, while American locomotive practice could be seen in Canada, South America, and even in parts of the British Empire; for New Zealand, Australia, and South Africa occasionally bought American.

There was also considerable cross-fertilization. In the early twentieth century George Churchward, the locomotive superintendent of the Great Western Railway in England, designed a range of very distinctive locomotives that combined British, American and French features. From America he took the tapered boiler resting on a smokebox saddle that consisted of 2 castings, each containing one cylinder and half the smokebox saddle, and also the 2-6-0 wheel arrangement, which he used for the first British mixed-traffic locomotive. His leading 4-wheel truck was of French origin, his firebox was of an improved Belgian Belpaire type, and he paid great attention to providing wide,

smooth, internal steam passages, a fundamental improvement which he probably arrived at himself, although the proportions of chimney and blast-pipe, so important for good steaming, were derived from the theoretical work of the American Professor Goss. This new range of locomotives soon proved itself superior to those of other British railways, which eventually copied some of its features.

A sudden and wholesale adoption of American practice occurred in inter-war Russia, which had up to now been influenced mainly by Germany and Austria. There had been hints in the 1920s of the emergence of a new, Soviet, school of design, but this was cut short by the upheavals of the 1930s. A Soviet delegation visited the United States, an order was placed with Baldwin and Alco for 5 locomotives each, and the visiting Soviet engineers were arrested on their return, confined together with their drawing boards, and quickly produced designs for a 2-10-2 freight locomotive and its 'Josif Stalin' 2-8-4 passenger version. These, mass-produced in Soviet factories, were absolutely American both in fundamentals and details. After World War II, Soviet engineers helped the Chinese to introduce new locomotives of their own and the Chinese 'QJ' 2-10-2 had evident similarities with the postwar Soviet 'P36' 4-8-4 and 'LV' 2-10-2, which were themselves influenced by their American-style predecessors.

In Australia, the New South Wales Government Railways, after almost a century of British practice, built their own indigenous design during World War II. This was the Class '38' Pacific, intended for long runs without engine-change. In South Australia the inter-war years witnessed the phenomenon of new locomo-

Left: The final flowering of German steam locomotive design; passenger 4-6-2 locomotives in service at Osnabrück in the 1960s.

Below left: One of several hundred '141R'-type locomotives exported from the United States and Canada to the war-torn French Railways of the late 1940s.

Right: A 'P36'-type 4-8-4 of the Soviet Railways leaving Leningrad.

Below right: A 'QJ' 2-10-2 of the Chinese Railways, a design still being built in the 1980s. Its similarities with the Soviet locomotive pictured above result from the presence of Soviet engineers in China during the 1950s.

tives that were twice as big as their predecessors, designed in Australia, built in Britain, but American in style. A final class, mixed-traffic 4-8-4s, clearly imitated the Pennsylvania Railroad's 4-4-4-4s with their sharp-nosed air-smoothed cladding.

Another case of British-built locomotives taking an American form was a number of 2-8-0s built for railways in the Andes. These lines had been originally engineered by Americans, who specified an American-built 2-8-0 design. These were built by United States locomotive companies, but after World War II further orders were placed in Britain, the British manufacturers simply copying the American design. Similarly, in World War I, British works built French-design engines for France.

South African locomotives in the twentieth century were recognizably South African, although mainly built in Britain. This was because design work was by South African engineers, who evolved their own style, and because large-diameter boilers, with chimney and other boiler fittings of low profile, had a distinctive air on 3-foot 6-inch gauge tracks.

Had it not been for the advent of the diesel, world steam locomotive development after World War II would have probably produced a trend toward the American style, especially with the good impression made by the many American-built 2-8-2 locomotives exported during (and soon after) the war. These included the '141R' class for France, the '59' class for New South Wales, and many 'MacArthur' engines for other countries. The American emphasis on ease of maintenance was very much appreciated in postwar conditions. Even British postwar designs included American labor-saving devices such as rocking grates, and a preference for outside cylinders and valve gears with their easier access.

Left: A Soviet 'Josif Stalin' locomotive enters Kiev. This Russian inter-war design was entirely American-inspired.

Above right: An inter-war German Pacific of the lightweight 'O3' type, now preserved.

Right: The British and American tradition in Australia. A late nineteenth-century British 4-6-0 (on the left) and a United States-built 'MacArthur' 2-8-2 at Newcastle, in New South Wales.

The Inter-War Electrifications

It is perhaps surprising that the railways of America and Europe did not electrify more than they did in the inter-war years. In many cases there were sound economic reasons for continuing with steam traction, and the Depression of the 1930s deferred many schemes, but inertia on the part of railway managements and their political or financial overseers was a large factor.

In terms of proportion of total mileage electrified, Italy led the way. Coal was expensive in that country, there was a highly developed tradition of electrical engineering, and electrified railways created precisely the kind of image Mussolini sought for his regime. The result was not only a high mileage of electrified line, but the development of hydro-electric generating schemes. Passenger services could be accelerated and luxurious, extra-fare, electric train-sets were introduced, one of which averaged 102mph on trial over the Florence to Milan route in 1939.

3000V DC was the Italian system, marginally superior to the French 1500V which was used for the inter-war electrifications from Paris to Toulouse and Bordeaux and the shorter length from Paris to Le Mans. The USSR began with 1500V but later changed to 3000V, the higher voltage enabling sub-stations to be placed farther apart and, in practice, allowing more power to be supplied; an important factor when several trains were drawing current from the same stretch of overhead conductor. In Germany, where locomotive coal was plentiful and the steam locomotive well-liked, there were short electrifications in the mountainous areas, especially Bavaria, and the north-south trunk line from Magdeburg to Leipzig was also electrified.

But as might be expected, it was countries with ample hydro-electric sources and steeply graded lines that gained most. In Sweden the 280-mile Lapland Railway, carrying heavy iron-ore traffic over difficult terrain, was electrified in 1923, and 2 years later the Stockholm to Göteborg main line was converted. Other conversions followed. In Switzerland and Austria progress was also fast. Indeed, the Swiss electrical engineering industry with its advanced companies like Oerlikon and Brown Boveri made many advances in electric locomotive technology, including a system for transmitting power from motor to axle that for the first time made it possible for electric locomotives to run at very high speeds; an important innovation.

Sweden, Germany, Austria and Switzerland all chose 15,000V AC, which had the advantage of widely spaced sub-stations, less loss in transmission, and lighter conductor wires, but required each locomotive to carry a rectifier to provide the direct current required by the traction motors. At the other end of the voltage

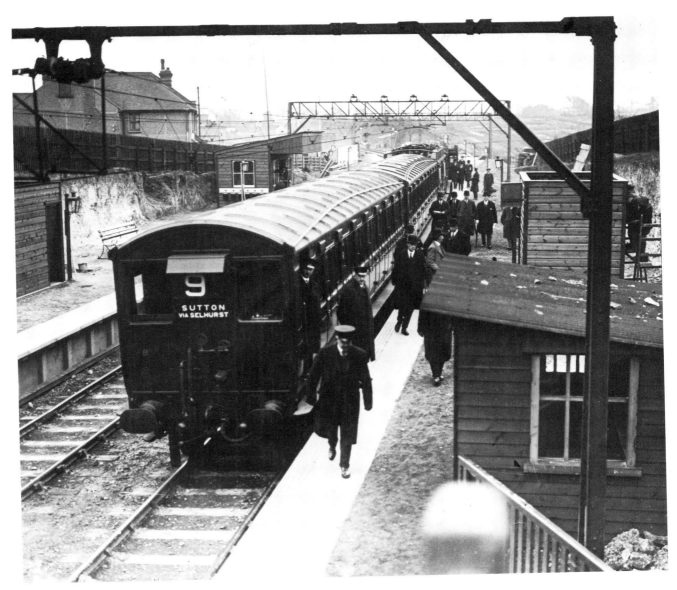

Below left: A Great Northern Railroad 3300hp electric locomotive of 1927, hauling the *Cascadian* passenger train. The shrouded headlamp indicates that this picture was taken during World War II.

Right: An early (1925) Southern Railway electrification. This line used overhead transmission, technically more promising than the third-rail system that the SR finally standardized.

Below right: Government money encouraged the LNER to electrify its trans-Pennine line, but World War II delayed completion. The original locomotive, pictured here, had no work and in 1947 was loaned to the Netherlands Railways for 5 years.

scale was the Southern Railway in England which, alone of the 4 British companies, pursued the electrification schemes with great enthusiasm.

The SR was primarily a passenger-carrying railway, and most of its passengers were short-distance. Heavy traffic flows, the need for high power outputs to guarantee rapid acceleration from frequent stops, and the new company's quest for a modern image, were clear recommendations for electrification, and the SR went ahead, using the existing London to Wimbledon scheme as a basis. This was a third-rail system, with a fairly low voltage. Such a system is very suited to commuter railways, for the traction motors can take their current more or less directly from the conductor rail, with no need for heavy auxiliary equipment. Moreover, the third rail with its wide cross-section is well adapted to carrying the powerful current needed when closely spaced trains are accelerating from stations.

The SR electrification provided a network of electrified lines to the south of London, and then began to embrace longer-distance routes, from London to Brighton and later, from London to Portsmouth. The third-rail low-voltage system was less suited to these distances, but was accepted for the sake of uniformity. The SR found that electrification, enabling a faster and more frequent service, attracted new passengers to the railway (a phenomenon that would later be known as the 'sparks effect'), and land prices rose in the area served by Southern Electric. Although a handful of electric locomotives were built for freight, Southern Electric passenger services were provided by electric trains, with one or more multiple units (groups of cars, some powered, with a cab at each end) coupled together to form a train of the required length. Elsewhere in Britain, schemes were drawn up, but capital was not forthcoming to make them a reality. The LNER finally started work on 2 schemes, but these were interrupted by the war.

Throughout the world, conversion of heavy-traffic suburban lines was typically the first move in the electrification process. In the USSR, the Moscow and Leningrad networks were electrified

in the 1930s. In India, 2 routes out of Bombay were converted. In South Africa, schemes at Cape Town and Durban were started in the 1920s, the former at 1500V and the latter at 3000V. When the Witwatersrand area was later converted at 3000V, that voltage was established as the future standard. In Australia, electrification began of the Sydney and Melbourne networks, both at 1500V.

These suburban schemes later became parts of longer-distance electrifications. Indeed, in the smaller countries like Holland and Belgium 2 suburban networks could meet and provide an inter-city electrification, as happened with Brussels-Antwerp and Amsterdam-The Hague-Rotterdam. In the United States, the Pennsylvania Railroad's suburban electrification out of New York was a stimulus for the conversion of the main line down to Washington and Harrisburg, a scheme whose last section was ready in 1939. Before then, in 1934, the first of the classic 'GG1'

Above left: The finally completed LNER electrification; a train from Sheffield enters Manchester.

Left: One of the original trains of the inter-war Brussels suburban electrification.

Above right: One of the long-lived suburban trains introduced in the 1920s for the Melbourne electrification.

Right: Originally bought in Britain in the mid-1920s for use by the National Harbours Board in Montreal, this type 'Z4a' electric locomotive was later acquired by Canadian National Railways, and is still used in Montreal commuter operations.

semi-streamlined electric locomotives had been assembled; the forerunner of a 139-strong class that would handle all the heavy passenger traffic of this line until the 1970s.

Because of the high capital cost of electrification, it was suitable only where traffic was dense or where electrification was the best solution to technical problems. In North America, traffic density was low except on a few lines in the east, but there were heavily graded lines in alpine terrain in the northwest. Here the Milwaukee Railroad electrified 656 miles and the Great Northern 74 miles, of their transcontinental lines although these sections were 'de-electrified' after World War II.

American electrification was characterized not only by its sparsity, but also by the variety of different systems employed. The Pennsylvania Railroad scheme used 11,000V AC, with Westinghouse supplying the electrical equipment. Westinghouse's competitor, General Electric, equipped the Milwaukee and Great Northern electrifications, the latter at 11,000V but the former at 3000V DC. The Virginian Railway also used 11,000V for the conversion of 134 miles of its coal-hauling main line.

United States electric locomotives also took a variety of forms. The pre-World War I Norfolk and Western electric locomotives used 3-phase motors, which were technically convenient but allowed the locomotive to operate at only 2 speeds (14mph and 28mph). On the Milwaukee Railroad huge bipolar locomotives could be seen, contrasting starkly with the rough-hewn poles that carried the conductor wires.

The Coming of the Diesel

In a fast-moving age, it is strange that the diesel locomotive took longer than the steam locomotive to gain acceptance. It is less strange that the first attempts were built before Rudolph Diesel had invented his engine, for the diesel was only an improved version of the oil engine. A British 12hp 4-wheel dockyard locomotive built in 1894 is regarded as the pioneer, built for British government arsenals. Later, gasoline motors were tried, and but for World War I, the Trans-Australian Railway would have acquired a gasoline-electric locomotive, in which the engine drove a generator that in turn supplied the traction motors, as in the later diesel-electrics.

Elsewhere in the world, a Swedish short line acquired some diesel-electric rail cars, and in 1912 the Prussian State Railways tried to operate the world's first mainline diesel locomotive, and failed for a number of reasons, including a chronic inability to start the engine.

Meanwhile, in the United States, the internal combustion engine was being used to power rail cars, offering reduced operating costs for light-traffic branch lines. The McKeen rail car, bought by several lines, used a gasoline engine and chain drive. Then the General Electric Company, inspired by a successful British rail car which used an 85hp gasoline engine to drive a generator, produced its own gas-electric rail car, of which about 90 were sold before World War I. From this rail-car design General Electric created three 400hp gas-electric locomotives for the Dan Patch short line, which used them successfully for the passenger trains.

Soon after the Russian Revolution, Lenin approved the building of experimental diesel locomotives as a way to revolutionize Soviet Railways. One of these, sponsored by the leading Russian railway engineer, Georgii Lomonosov, was built in Germany and was a 1200hp diesel-electric, while another was built in Leningrad, using a Vickers engine intended for a submarine. Both were finished in November 1924, but Lomonosov's worked satisfactorily while the other did not. The Lomonosov locomotive, a 2-10-2 rigid-frame machine, may therefore be regarded as the world's first successful mainline diesel. The USSR subsequently built several similar units, which worked in Central Asia until the 1950s.

One of the Russian designers, Alphonse Lipets, emigrated and joined the American Locomotive Company, or Alco. This firm had co-operated with General Electric in the construction of some diesel-electric yard locomotives. One of these, No 1000, which was built in 1925 for the Central of New Jersey Railroad, is regarded as the first commercially successful diesel-electric locomotive in the United States and was destined for a long life. By 1928 Alco was interested in manufacturing higher-power diesels, and its first order came from the New York Central, which took three 750hp units for light-traffic lines. Even after 1937, when new work-rules made it difficult to use 1-man crews on yard diesel locomotives, they were an attractive proposition because they could work almost 24 hours daily; that is, a single diesel could replace 2 steam locomotives. For most of the 1930s, therefore, Alco found a healthy market for its diesel yard locomotives. These usually had engines of 300hp or 600hp, although Alco's

Left: One of the celebrated 'GG1' electric locomotives of the Pennsylvania Railroad leaves Washington with a train for New York. Introduced in the 1930s, the 'GG1' class served this main line for 4 decades.

Below left: An electric locomotive supplied by Metropolitan Vickers for the Great Indian Peninsula Railway's electrification out of Bombay. As with many other electric locomotives of the 1920s, the drive is through jackshafts and connecting rods.

Right: A 1933 diesel-electric rail car, tried by the LMS Railway between Warwick and Northampton.

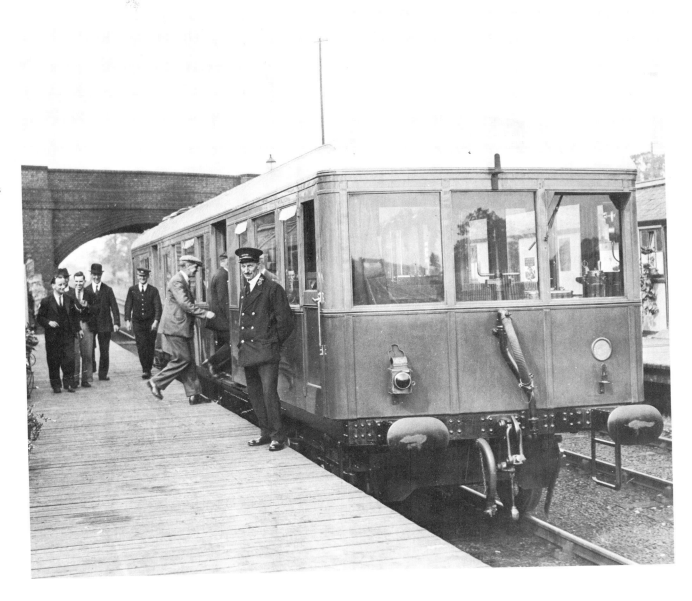

introduction of the turbocharger consequently enabled the latter to be rerated to 900hp.

In 1940 Alco built the first dual-service diesel locomotive. This rode on two 6-wheel trucks and had 2 engines, producing 2000hp. An immediate success on the New Haven Railroad, where it hauled passenger trains in the day and freights at night, it led to the first road-switcher, which combined the functions of a mainline and yard locomotive.

Meanwhile General Motors (GM) the automobile company, bought up the Electro-Motive Corporation, which marketed and designed gas-electric rail cars. It also bought a maker of diesel engines, and with this combination of experience entered the diesel locomotive market. GM provided power for the *Burlington Zephyr* and other streamliners, and also began to make diesel switchers. It insisted on producing a standard design, allowing no variations, in order to contain the diesel locomotive's rather high capital cost. In 1939 GM built a diesel-electric freight locomotive consisting of 4 units and having an output of 5400hp. It demonstrated this over many American railroads, which were impressed by the convenience of its use. Orders began to arrive for the production version, known as the 'FT,' and General Motors was further helped by the war, because federal regulations named it as the only builder of mainline diesel locomotives.

Meanwhile, other countries were experimenting with diesel traction. In Britain the GWR built its fleet of diesel rail cars, while

manufacturers tried to interest railway companies in diesel locomotives. Armstrong-Whitworth built some satisfactory diesel
trains for Brazil and the Argentine, and Beardmore powered a
diesel-electric locomotive for Canadian National Railways. The
English Electric Company developed a 300hp diesel engine for
railway use, and this powered a very successful design of yard
locomotive that was used in Britain, exported to the Netherlands,
and forms the basis of today's BR 'O8' type yard locomotive.

A theoretical drawback of the diesel locomotive was the difficulty of converting the high-speed rotary action of the engine to
the slow revolutions of the driving wheels. Using electricity as a
medium solved this problem, but necessitated the provision of a
generator; in effect, this meant that 1 locomotive carried 2 power
units, which added to cost and weight. Methods of mechanical or
hydro-mechanical transmission were worked out for low-power
locomotives and, in Germany, hydraulic transmissions for
powerful locomotives were devised. They were used in the
record-breaking *Flying Hamburger* twin-unit train, and in a
1500hp mainline locomotive built in 1935. Germany also built
diesel rail cars and diesel yard locomotives in large numbers, but
they became an embarrassment in World War II because of
limited oil supplies.

Left: A French National Railways
fast-diesel railcar unit in the Paris to
Lille service.

Below left: An 'E8' 2250hp diesel-
electric passenger locomotive,
supplied by General Motors to the
Seaboard Railroad in the 1950s.

Right: An 'E7' 2000hp passenger
diesel-electric locomotive built in
the 1950s by General Motors for the
Burlington Railroad.

Below right: The General Motors
4-unit freight diesel-electric
demonstrator locomotive of 1939.

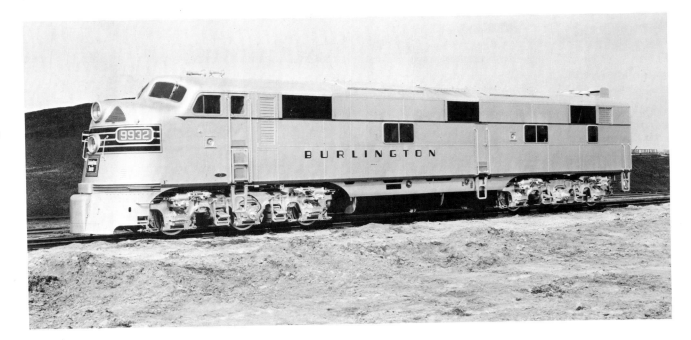

THERE'S SOMETHING NEW IN THE PICTURE

The "Best Friend of Charleston" was the first locomotive entirely built in this country—for the South Carolina Railroad, now part of the Southern Railway System.

Daily movement of a staggering quantity of oil from New Orleans to the Eastern States is the No. 1 war job of the Southern Railway. The Southern assigns its fleet of General Motors Diesel freight locomotives as the key motive power to expedite this important flow.

There will be something new in the farm and industrial pictures too. For there will be GM Diesels ready to serve wherever America needs power.

OUT of every war has grown a new era in transportation. This one is no exception. The pattern of that new era had been set, even before this war, by the General Motors Diesel Locomotive. And its Leadership in the Peace to come is forecast in the way this locomotive is today meeting the challenges of war.

GM GENERAL MOTORS DIESEL POWER

LOCOMOTIVES.....................ELECTRO-MOTIVE DIVISION, La Grange, Ill

ENGINES..150 to 2000 H.P...CLEVELAND DIESEL ENGINE DIVISION, Cleveland, Ohio

ENGINES.....15 to 250 H.P......DETROIT DIESEL ENGINE DIVISION, Detroit, Mich

Left: A wartime poster in which General Motors staked its claim to the postwar dieselization of United States railroads.

Below left: Alco was the other main contender for the United States diesel market, and was strong in the road-switcher type, as exemplified by this New York Central Railroad unit.

Above right: One of the scores of posters issued by railways of the belligerent countries in World War II and intended, usually, to maintain the railways' reputation for service and patriotism amid wartime difficulties.

Right: A shipment of new Churchill tanks on the LMS Railway in 1942.

Diesel rail cars were also developed in France. The most spectacular were the Bugatti high-speed rail cars, covering the Paris to Deauville run of 137 miles in 2 hours. A variety of rail cars were built, some for fast service and some for lightly used branches. A few experimental diesel locomotives were also tried, but were not outstanding.

Frichs, a Danish company, scored a modest success with its mainline diesel-electric locomotives supplied to the Thai railways. They worked in Thailand for more than 2 decades, and were popular because they burned oil rather than the high-quality teak consumed by Thai steam locomotives.

The Lines behind the Lines

The British railways had a dress rehearsal for war in 1938, when the Munich Crisis saw them running evacuation specials out of the cities as well as troop trains, all without disrupting normal services. In Britain, and to a large extent in the United States, the war showed how much spare capacity the railways possessed. Even the evacuation from Dunkirk, which meant the spontaneous generation of hundreds of troop trains, was accomplished by the British railways without any reduction of normal services, apart from those around 2 of the southern ports.

A Railway Executive Committee of senior British railway managers, similar to that which had been so successful in the previous war, was established before war started, and worked well. Once again the railways seemed to perform more efficiently in wartime than in peacetime, although the difference was not now so marked. What was new was that in World War II the railways were expected to continue their work under air bombardment and with a nightly blackout.

An early sign of war was the fitting of locomotives with gas detection panels that would change color should the train pass through a cloud of poisonous gas. Station lights were kept switched off and white lines painted along platform edges in partial compensation. Dim blue bulbs replaced the white lights in passenger vehicles, and opaque black borders were painted on windows. Heavy bombing started in 1940 and in total, about 400 railwaymen were killed on duty. In early May 1941, 7 of the London terminals were out of action for some time. After a relaxation in 1943, the flying bombs and rockets began to fall in 1944, but though these were nerve-wracking, they caused little damage to the railways.

The British railways handed some of their locomotives to the War Department for service overseas and in return, they later received standard war-built locomotives. The Stanier LMS freight 2-8-0 was chosen as the wartime production type, and was built in several workshops. Meanwhile, the Ministry of Supply was designing its own locomotives for military service; these

took into account the need to save metal and working hours in their construction, and to cope with difficult operating conditions on the continent of Europe, where most were expected to work. A small 0-6-0 saddle tank was also built, and a few units of a heavy freight locomotive of the unusual (for Britain) 2-10-0 wheel arrangement. Later, the railways had the use of the United States Transportation Corps 2-8-0 until it was needed to serve the American Army in Europe. This was a simple locomotive, with a tendency to suffer boiler explosions when in the hands of unwary crews.

The British government ordered from American builders several hundred 2-8-2 locomotives of traditional United States design, but with some British features. This was the celebrated 'MacArthur' class, of which most went to India (where they still work), and others to the Trans-Iran Railway. The latter, which ran from the Persian Gulf to the Caspian, was taken over by the British and Russians after Hitler's invasion of the USSR. The Russians operated its northern part and the British (after 1944, the Americans) its southern part. It was an important route for

supplying the Russians, especially after its very difficult operating conditions had been alleviated by the introduction of United States diesel locomotives.

Hitler's invasion of Russia in 1941 was hampered by his reliance on road transport. Having expected the Red Army to collapse because of the allegedly defective railway system, he discovered that his own advance was held back because his highway transport could not cope with the inadequate Russian roads and too little provision had been made for the Wehrmacht's rail transport. Russian locomotives had been withdrawn or demolished and, having few locomotives of the right gauge, the Germans were unable to adequately supply their drives against Moscow and Leningrad.

French, Dutch and German railways suffered badly during the war. In the case of France, bomb damage was supplemented by the far more precise destruction wreaked by the Resistance.

The United States railroads, having learned a hard lesson in World War I, co-ordinated their activities so well that there was no need for another government takeover. They easily handled the upsurge of traffic in the east when German submarines brought coastal shipping to a virtual standstill, and they coped with the huge burden of troop and supply movement as the nation mobilized. Line capacity was ample, but passenger cars were sometimes short, so troops had to be often moved in converted boxcars. Military supply railways were the concern of the Corps of Engineers until 1942, when the United States Transportation Corps was formed. Like the British, the Americans took their own railway operating units with them in the European campaign. This, again, was a repetition of World War I practice. There was a change, however: fronts were not static in World War II, so there was no need for narrow-gauge front railways.

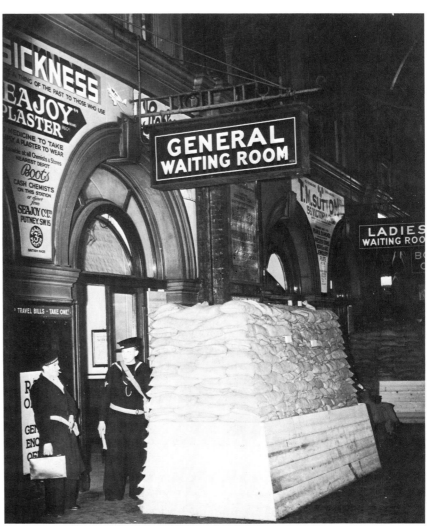

Above left: One of the United States Army's standard 2-8-0 locomotives. This unit found its way to India, but most were used in liberated Europe.

Left: A photograph made by a German engineer officer on taking over a locomotive depot in the Russian campaign. Russian demolition typically took the form, as here, of explosive charges in the firebox and behind the cylinders.

Above: Moorgate station on the London Underground system, after a bomb attack.

Right: A sandbag blast screen at a London terminus.

PART 4

NEW DIRECTIONS: 1945 TO THE PRESENT

Reorganization and Modernization

No railway system emerged from World War II in total ruin, but the western lines of the USSR had suffered badly, and in the Netherlands the railways were in such a poor state that the government decided not to simply restore them, but to completely rebuild on the basis of electric traction. In Germany, too, destruction was widespread because the Allied bombing had been directed against a system that was already feeling the effect of wartime scarcities.

In Britain, actual damage had been small, but the arrears of accumulated maintenance and replacement were enormous. To a much lesser extent, the American railroads were also suffering from the effects of heavy wartime traffic imposed on lines which had not been properly maintained or renewed because of the wartime scarcities.

It was in these run-down conditions that the railways of North America and Europe had to face the onslaught of renewed competition. The war, far from holding back the development of highway and air transport, had done much to stimulate them. Moreover, postwar governments for one reason or another decided to invest huge sums in highways and airports. In Europe, however, where the importance of a healthy railway system was usually recognized, some governments did legislate to prevent truck transport driving the railways to the wall. Such legislation typically imposed limits on the number of licensed highway operators and restricted their share of the traffic.

In North America and Britain the railroads were allowed to languish. In the United States, federal highway construction

Previous spread: A French National Railways high-speed train prototype, which reached 190mph on this trial run near Bordeaux.

Above: As the law prescribed, notices of the intention to nationalize the British railways were displayed at all stations.

Left: Usk Castle at midnight, 31 December 1947, ready to take the first British Railways train from Paddington Station.

Right: A former LMS Railway locomotive receives its new British Railways number and lettering in 1948.

gave considerable advantage to the truckers, while an enormous program of works by the Army's engineers created virtually new waterway systems along the eastern seaboard, and also several river systems were refurbished. At the same time, continental distances, the availability of cheap surplus transport aircraft, and the eagerness of civic authorities to finance new airports, soon had their effect on railroad passenger traffic. In Britain, highway operators (both passenger and freight) benefitted from the new motorways which were built and other road improvements, while paying very little toward their construction and upkeep through taxes and license fees. In both countries the railways were hampered by regulations directed against competitive rate-cutting and so began to suffer.

By the late 1940s it was clear that the railways of Britain and North America were in decline and the failure of governments to remedy this by ensuring a fairer competitive framework implies that this decline was quite acceptable to those governments. Neither in Britain nor the United States were the railways held high in public esteem. Apart from the cardinal sin of appearing old-fashioned, they suffered from citizens' unpleasant memories of recent wartime travel.

While legislation tied one hand firmly behind the railways' backs, the powerful railway trade unions gripped tightly the other hand. Thus the American railroads' natural reaction to competition; re-equipment to provide better service at lower cost, met unnatural obstacles. Introducing diesel power should have brought some reduced labor costs by eliminating locomotive firemen, but the struggle on this issue was long drawn-out and by the late 1980s still not properly resolved. As was so often the case, the various railroad companies failed to present a united front; this had been crucial in 1935, when they had not supported the Burlington Railroad in its contention that the diesel 'Zephyrs' did not need firemen. The Canadian Pacific strike of 1957 and the American rail strike of 1963 emphasized that the locomotive fireman would be drawing his pay for many more years. The 1963 strike did have an interesting outcome when the Florida East Coast Railroad (FEC) broke ranks and refused to accept union-imposed work-rules any longer; the FEC abolished firemen and other surplus train staff and went on to become one of the most efficient railroads and also one of the safest, despite occasional sabotage by its enemies.

Under union pressure, many states had legislated 'full-crew laws,' by which railroads were compelled to attach a minimum number of workers to all trains operating in a given state. This meant that trains which, technically, could be handled by a single man had to have a complement of 5 or 7. Meanwhile, steam-age pay systems were not allowed to wither. A full day's work for a locomotive crew was still 100 miles. This had been fair enough in the days when trains only averaged 10-20mph, but in the 1950s it meant that fast trains needed to change crews approximately every 2 hours. Whereas a single truck driver might take his cargo 600 miles in a day, a train moving 600 miles might need to pay a day's wage to about 40 crew-men.

In the face of such waste, the technical advantage of steel wheels running on steel rails was of little avail. High-cost operation, the decline of heavy industries which traditionally supplied the railroads with their bulk traffic, managerial inertia partly due to the labor and legislative obstacles that crushed any initiative; all combined to produce declining traffic, line closures and general depression in the railroad industry. In 1916, the peak year for United States railroads, railwaymen represented 4 percent of the American labor force, the railroads carried 75 percent of all freight and 98 percent of passengers. But in 1966, although

freight traffic was double that of 1916, it was only 43 percent of the total. Passenger traffic was only 50 percent that of 1916, even though the American population had doubled, and railroad workers represented only 1 percent of total workers.

Railroad bankruptcies and amalgamations were one result. Among amalgamations, that of the rival New York Central and Pennsylvania railroads, joined later by the New Haven Railroad, only made things worse, and the new company, Penn Central, soon collapsed. This bankruptcy, and the perilous state of other eastern railroads, did at last persuade the federal government that something needed to be done. The Consolidated Rail Corporation (Conrail) was formed in 1976 under federal auspices to combine the lines of the Penn Central, Erie-Lackawanna, Reading, Central of New Jersey, Lehigh Valley, and Lehigh and Hudson River railroads. With a small measure of co-operation from the unions, some sensible management, and government sympathy and finance, Conrail did begin to reduce costs and produce net revenue, enabling it to be offered to private purchasers as a going concern. Earlier, federal intervention had created Amtrak, to operate a national system of passenger train services.

Compared to other countries, the United States railroad system was organizationally fluid. Mergers were always under discussion; those that became reality in the postwar decades included the combination of the Burlington, Great Northern, Northern Pacific, and Spokane, Portland and Seattle into the new powerful and prosperous Burlington Northern Railroad. The once rival Seaboard Railroad and Atlantic Coast Line merged to form the Seaboard Coast Line which later, as part of the CSX System, joined with the Baltimore and Ohio, Chesapeake and Ohio, Louisville and Nashville and other railroads. The Norfolk Southern combined under a single management the 2 giants Nor-

Streamliner

"CITY OF LOS ANGELES"

Swiftly, smoothly . . . past the twinkling lights of towns . . . verdant valleys . . . rolling hills. Train travel is stimulating, pleasurable. On the "City of Los Angeles" it reaches a high peak of enjoyment.

Daily . . . between Chicago and Los Angeles.

COACH OR PULLMAN

UNION PACIFIC RAILROAD

Left: The Union Pacific Railroad resumes normal service.

Above right: The New York Central Railroad looks forward with confidence to the future of its passenger service.

Above far right: By the late 1950s the North American railroads realized they could not beat the airlines on long runs, so they began to portray transcontinental train trips as holidays.

Right: An example of wasteful practice; at the end of its run a Canadian LRC train, quite capable of self-propelled movement, is allocated a yard locomotive and crew to take it to the maintenance tracks.

folk and Western and the Southern. In the same period, several companies disappeared through bankruptcy, including the New York, Ontario and Western, the Milwaukee, and the Rock Island railroads. At the same time a number of new short lines appeared, often taking over sections of bankrupt companies.

By the 1980s, some easing of the United States railroads' situation was evident. Deregulation, and in particular the Staggers Act, freed the railroads of much federal supervision. It became easier to close lines and withdraw services. Above all, the railroads regained much of their old freedom in rate-setting, which

enabled them to respond more flexibly to price competition. The unions began to make concessions with selected acceptance of 2-man crews for certain trains and an agreement to dispense with cabooses.

In Britain, the 4 big companies became the state-owned British Railways in 1948, later British Rail (BR). Nationalization occurred, however, not because the government favored railways but because it disfavored private ownership. Railways were mishandled in the postwar decades, largely because of a reluctance to grasp nettles. Unwilling to accept, as in continental

Europe, that railways were a public service worthy of subsidization, yet at the same time unwilling to accept that railways should abandon loss-making services, successive British governments had no clear-cut railway policy but seemed to expect BR to both make a profit and provide uneconomic services. As the railways staggered from crisis to crisis, the governments, anxious to be seen doing something, made successive organizational changes that did little except unsettle management and clients. Once, in the early 1960s, at a time when road transport was exceptionally strong politically, the government decided that profit should come first. The Beeching Report followed in 1963, after which thousands of miles of route and thousands of stations were closed, and an effort was made to provide modern freight services. As usual when essential decisions are taken too late, the policy was taken too far, and with an obsessional zeal the BR administration proceeded to close not only loss-making facilities but also lines and stations which, given time and effort, could have contributed to revenue.

After this period of sacrifice, BR settled down to digest its ill-prepared (because they had been hurried) modernization plans. It still faced a number of hindrances. The press, which was mainly hostile to nationalized industries, was so keen to condemn BR that useful criticism was swamped by a sea of petty, and often fabricated aspersions. The railways had no real representative in the government. Ostensibly they were the responsibility of the Minister of Transport, but the latter, apart from averaging barely 2 years in office before being transferred elsewhere, headed a department that was more interested in road transport than in rail. On top of all this BR, unlike the previous companies was not allowed to raise capital. It had to, in the preceding decades, rely on government money, which was rarely forthcoming without protracted negotiation and interference, so pro-

jects that could have returned investment within a few years were simply not attempted. In the 1980s British railway investment per mile of route was about 25 percent of that of Belgium.

From time to time there was talk of privatization, but the problem of persuading private investors to purchase BR's loss-making businesses as well as the potentially profitable, was a deterrent. However, the Japanese National Railways were denationalized in 1987, and a few other countries were exploring the idea.

Triumph of the Diesel

After the war ended more and more United States railroads decided to stop placing orders for steam locomotives. They had been impressed by the performance of the General Motors diesel locomotives produced in limited quantities during the war and, free of government control over purchases, aimed to eliminate the steam locomotive. General Motors, benefitting from its privileged position as monopoly supplier during the war, expanded its output but soon began to face competition. Alco, the steam locomotive company, partnered General Electric to become the second-biggest builder, while the 2 other big locomotive companies, Baldwin and Lima, tried but failed to make a success of diesel traction. Meanwhile, Fairbanks Morse used an American Navy opposed-piston diesel-engine design to power its 'Trainmaster,' a high-horsepower (2400hp) unit which failed to make much impact thanks to General Motors' dominant market position.

General Electric, which was also an independent producer of its own designs, specialized in a 44-ton yard and branchline diesel locomotive which was an exceptionally low-cost unit because American work-rules allowed a 1-man crew for diesel locomotives of less than 45 tons. After leaving its partnership with Alco, General Electric introduced its own mainline diesel

Above left: A modern Australian National Railways diesel locomotive in Victoria, hauling an interstate freight to Adelaide.

Left: A British Rail Class '50' diesel locomotive, garnished with the livery of BR's Network South East. Class '50' was a sophisticated AC/DC design which has given good results, but withdrawal of the class began in the late 1980s because suitable duties were diminishing and maintenance costs were quite high.

Right: One of the General Motors Class '59' diesel locomotives used over BR track by the Foster Yeoman quarrying company.

Above: Gas turbine locomotives of the Union Pacific Railroad await their freight duties at Cheyenne, Wyoming, in 1957.

Left: Locally built General Motors diesel locomotives in mineral train service on South African Railways.

Above right: A cab diesel unit leads one of the Santa Fe Railroad's transcontinental trains out of Chicago. The strikingly painted baggage car belongs to the Atlantic Coast Line Railroad.

Below right: An Alco diesel locomotive, one of hundreds of United States exports, at work on the Spanish National Railways.

locomotive in 1960, the 'U25B' 2500hp road-switcher. The result of years of research, the 'U25B' had electronic controls, a body that was largely maintenance-free, and had pressurized (therefore dust-free) equipment compartments. Its excellence enabled General Electric to win a foothold in the market despite General Motors' dominance. For a time Alco's Canadian subsidiary, Montreal Locomotive, continued to build Alco designs, as did the Indian Railways' diesel locomotive plant set up earlier by Alco, but the American market and export trade was held by General Motors and General Electric from now on.

Initially, the mainline locomotive market was dominated by the 'cab' type of locomotive, in which the body was the full width of the locomotive and was streamlined; 'A' units were provided with a streamlined cab while 'B' units were cabless and intended to be attached to 'A' units. It was this facility of adding units to form a multiple-unit locomotive controlled by a single crew, plus the high availability of the diesel, that made it so popular among railroad operators. Later, the more functional road-switcher (in which the machinery was enclosed in a narrow hood, with external inspection walkways) superseded the cab units. Horsepowers varied from 1200 to 3600 per unit, although the UP bought some locomotives of 5000hp.

In many cases, the diesel locomotive was a cost-saving innovation which enabled managements to put off, for a few more years, long-needed changes, and this was part of the reason for the

rapidity of its adoption. Steam locomotives were written off needlessly early and by the mid-1950s, the coal-hauling Norfolk and Western Railroad was the only major American railroad still faithful to steam, a stronghold that was soon breached. The locomotive builders then switched to more powerful units, in order to create a second-generation market. They also benefitted from a trade in exports, typically with countries supplied with the necessary dollars by American or international finance institutions.

In many cases the diesel locomotive was oversold. Whereas in American conditions it usually had substantial operating and economic advantages over the steam locomotive, this was not necessarily true everywhere. Many Third World railways, whose governments had been attracted by the sales talk of American corporations, found themselves saddled with fleets of diesels that were largely unserviceable, as soon as they had run off their initial mileages. Shortage of spare parts, of skilled engineers and of proper maintenance facilities contributed to this situation.

In the more developed countries, the American builders often set up their own works, or licensed overseas builders to produce their designs. General Motors of Canada built GM designs for the Canadian railways, while Montreal Locomotive built Alco types. In Sweden, Nohab stopped building steam locomotives in favor of diesels incorporating GM technology, and so did 2 Belgian companies. In Australia, Clyde Engineering built its own ver-

Above left: A German, Krupp-built, diesel locomotive heading one of the trains of the Indonesian National Railways in 1972.

Left: A General Motors 'E7' diesel-electric, as supplied for passenger service to many United States railroads, including the Boston and Maine Railroad, as pictured here.

Above right: One of a class of very high horsepower (5000hp) freight diesel-electrics built for the Union Pacific Railroad by General Electric in the 1960s.

sions of GM designs while Goodwin produced what were essentially Alco locomotives. GM designs were also constructed in South Africa.

In much of Europe, however, American locomotives were excluded. The German diesel locomotive industry, building on past experience, evolved its own range of designs, many of which used hydraulic instead of electric transmission. Such transmissions dispensed with the need to carry heavy electric generators on each locomotive, but eventually it was found that the advantage of this was, for mainline units, more than outweighed by heavier maintenance expenses. In France and Italy, too, home industry produced its own designs, whereas the Spanish National Railways preferred to buy Alco or German designs. Russia went its own way, having absorbed American technology from a few United States units imported at the end of the war.

Some railways adopted policies of massive and rapid dieselization while others planned to replace the steam locomotive gradually. Some American lines, British Railways, and many Third World railways came into the first category while the French, German, South African and Australian railways were among those which took the more considered approach, introducing the diesel gradually.

British adoption of diesel power, introduced in the Modernisation Plan of 1955, stands as an example of how not to do it. BR had initially decided to remain with the steam locomotive, and dieselization proposals, being studied by the companies on the eve of nationalization were not pursued energetically. Then, seeing the success of dieselization in the United States, British Railways decided to make up for lost time. Domestic locomotive builders were gratified by massive orders for diesel locomotives of an excessively wide range of designs. The result was the multiplication of a few good but many inferior types. At the same time, the government ensured that no American builders would participate in this activity. This had the effect of excluding the most experienced diesel locomotive designers and builders from this transformation of British Railways, and contrasted with the former companies' longstanding willingness to seek overseas examples. The British approach to adopting diesel power was, therefore, an enormous misallocation of investment. Recently built steam locomotives were sent for scrap long before the end of their natural lives, and were soon joined by new, but defective, diesel locomotives. However, the French and German railways were more rational, conserving their steam locomotives while the main lines were being electrified, and thereby avoiding over-investment in diesels.

Among British successes was the development of the AC/DC locomotive, in which an alternator was fitted instead of a generator; modern electronics having eased the problem of converting AC (easier to produce) to DC (better for the traction motors). The prototype AC/DC unit was subsequently sold for study by Soviet engineers.

In the mid-1980s General Motors locomotives did at last move on British rails, when the quarrying company, Foster Yeoman, bought 4 advanced-technology units to haul its roadstone trains over BR track. These acquisitions had an invigorating effect on BR's traction engineers.

Postwar Electrification

The postwar decades were years of widespread electrification, however, this trend was hardly felt in the Americas. Indeed, in the United States there was a perceptible de-electrification as railroads discovered that after dieselization it made sense to replace their electric locomotives with diesel. By 1975 the electrified United States mileage, which had once reached 3100 miles, was down to less than 2000 miles, much of which was commuter line. The American situation, so out of order with the rest of the world, arose because electrification, which required an expensive infrastructure, was most economic on lines of high traffic density and such lines were rare in the United States, with its long, relatively low-traffic, routes.

The major United States electrification remained that of the former Pennsylvania Railroad line from New York to Washington and Harrisburg. Extension of this line to Pittsburgh was proposed but not attempted. Electric Amtrak passenger services were operated over this line, as they were over parts of the former New Haven Railroad's electrified route, but they were hauled by locomotives designed in Sweden, electric locomotive technology having languished in the United States from lack of orders.

Advanced technology was, however, employed on 2 specialized electric railroads. The first was the Muskingum Electric Railroad, opened in 1968 over 15 miles to transport coal to a generating station. It used high-voltage (25,000V AC) current which, at 60 cycles, corresponded to the public grid supply. The success of this line encouraged the building of another, longer, power station line. This was the 78-mile Black Mesa and Lake Powell Railroad in Arizona, which used the exceptionally high voltage of 50,000 AC. Both these lines used rectifier locomotives supplied by General Electric.

Another, longer, 50,000V electrification was undertaken in South Africa for the 535-mile Sishen to Saldanha ore-carrying railway. But, on the whole, it was the French who led the way in electric railway technology during the postwar decades. With over 2000 miles of electrified route open before the war, the SNCF had accumulated enough experience to plan the electrification of all its main routes, beginning with the Paris-Lyons-Mediterranean trunk line. At the same time the SNCF was successfully introducing the then-novel 25,000V AC system on the heavy-traffic Metz to Thionville line in eastern France.

It had always been realized that a high-voltage AC system would lower the cost of electrification, but the problem had been the need to rectify the current to make it suitable for the low-voltage DC traction motors of the locomotives. The postwar development of lightweight rectifiers provided a simple and fairly cheap solution for this. Next, the French used the system for the Paris to Lille electrification and then for all of their subsequent electrifications except for some that were continuations of older 1500V DC schemes.

In due course dual-current locomotives, capable of working over the old and new systems, were introduced to eliminate engine-changing where the 2 systems met. Later, several European railways introduced quadricurrent locomotives, capable of operating not only on the high-voltage AC system, but also on the older 1500V system of Holland and France, the 3000V system of Belgium, as well as the 15,000V system of the German railways – an important change.

Other railways that accepted the disadvantage of supporting 2 different electrification systems were Soviet Railways (which now has more electrified mileage than any other railway), and

Left: Sunnyside Yard, New York, in 1936. Amid various electric commuter services the New Haven Railroad's *Hellgate Express* (center) speeds toward Boston, passing, on the left, a 'GG1' electric of the Pennsylvania Railroad.

Above: One of the powerful high-voltage electric locomotives built for South African Railways.

Right: A turbotrain in Amtrak service speeds out of New York toward Albany. The oil crisis of the 1970s reduced the attraction of gas-turbine propulsion, which gives low maintenance costs but a quite high fuel consumption.

India; the French experience with 25,000V AC was so favorable that even though these countries had substantial DC mileages they willingly moved to the higher voltage. Others, including Italy at 3000V, the Scandinavian and central European block of countries using 15,000V AC, and New South Wales and Victoria at 1500V DC stayed with their old systems. Queensland, however, starting fresh with electrification in the 1970s, opted for 25,000V. In South Africa 3 systems coexisted, with the 25,000V and 50,000V systems for new electrifications and the 3000V system preserved on the older conversions.

British electrification was held back by shortage of investment funds, but this had the advantage that the first long mainline scheme, that from London to Birmingham, Liverpool, and Manchester was begun after the virtues of 25,000V AC had become apparent, and this system was adopted. Existing electrifications,

undertaken by the old companies, met varying fates. The Manchester to Sheffield scheme, over the Pennines, carried out by the LNER at 1500V, remained with that system, but eventually this route was closed. An LNER commuter scheme, from London to Shenfield, was changed from 1500V to the new system when it was extended. The dense third-rail network of the old Southern Railway was retained, and used for extensions into Kent and to Bournemouth, even though this system was not really suited to the longer-distance services.

The London to Manchester electrification not only reduced operating costs but enabled a new service of more frequent, faster, and brighter trains to be run, thereby attracting considerable new business to the railway. It was soon extended northward to Glasgow, where some commuter lines were also electrified. After this, despite the obvious success of electrification,

Left: The London to Southend suburban electrification of 1956. This was a project of the old LNER and was started at 1500 volts, but in 1960 it was changed to 25,000 volts.

Below left: A French National Railways quadricurrent locomotive hauling a Trans-European Express in 1964.

Right: A prototype electric train built for the Southern Region of British Railways in 1971. Some quite similar trains were later introduced in numbers, but the provision of smooth-riding rolling stock for the Region's intensive electric services was an extremely long-term project, possibly to be achieved by the end of the century.

Left: A *Gatwick Express*, linking London with nearby Gatwick Airport, in the charge of one of British Rail's electro-diesels (locomotives that normally run off the third-rail electric system but also have a diesel motor for use on non-electrified sections).

Above: Hamburg Station of the German Federal Railways, showing an Inter-City train behind a '103'-type electric locomotive and, at the other platform, a push-pull train propelled by a diesel locomotive.

Right: A French electric locomotive of the CC-7100 series on Swiss territory near Geneva. One of this class reached 206mph in 1958.

new schemes were more modest, comprising outer-suburban lines from London to Royston, near Cambridge, and from London to Bedford. The latter was completed in the early 1980s, and was followed by the electrification of a second route to Cambridge and an extension of existing electrification from London to Norwich. In this period too, the electrification of the East Coast main line from London to Edinburgh was begun, and this released high-speed trains for service elsewhere.

Twentieth century progress in electrical engineering was so rapid that electrification schemes adopted in one decade could be obsolescent in the next. There was a price to be paid for early innovation; the third-rail lines of southern England, once so progressive, are now technically disadvantageous. However, some of the innovations were applicable to locomotives rather than to whole systems. For example, new kinds of electronic control, thyristor control for AC units and chopper control for DC locomotives, enabled power to be increased in a continuous flow, rather than in a series of steps. Such a smooth transition helped to reduce wheelslip and therefore represented a real increase in a locomotive's tractive power. Electronics also gave birth to the current invertor, which enabled 3-phase AC traction motors to be used in place of the traditional DC type. The AC motor wears better in service, and a batch of current-invertor locomotives, Class '120,' was tried on German Railways. New third-rail trains, planned by British Rail for the 1990s, were also expected to incorporate this innovation.

Survival of Steam

On the eve of dieselization the locomotive works at Swindon in Britain conducted trials of different chimney and exhaust arrangements, revealing that with very careful design of drafting, the steam locomotive's efficiency could be noticeably enhanced. The problem had always been that the intermittent exhaust from the cylinders, used to provide a draft for the fire as it left the blast-pipe to exit through the chimney, was difficult to harness in such a way that it would provide a draft that was strong, steady, and unlikely to pull unburned coal particles from the grate. Various types of wide and double chimneys had appeared during the inter-war years, but perfection was still a long way off. An important step in the right direction was the postwar 'Giesl Ejector,' in which the exhaust steam was channeled through 7 nozzles, each aimed upward at a distinct part of the chimney orifice. Locomotives fitted with this device, recognizable by their elongated chimneys, extracted considerably more energy from the coal they burned. But the invention came too late to extend the life of steam traction in Britain and America, although it did find a role in central Europe, India, and China.

One of the countries where steam traction survived for a long time was the Argentine, and here the engineer L Porta continued the tradition of the Frenchman Chapelon by designing better blast-pipe and chimney arrangements, known as the Kylpor and Lempor chimneys. He also experimented with the combustion end of the locomotive, replacing the conventional firebox with a gas-producer grate in which the coal was kept at a fairly low temperature, gas being extracted from it and then burned at a higher level. These ideas were taken up by the South African Railways engineer P Wardale, under whose auspices an orthodox 4-8-4, No 3450, was rebuilt on Porta principles in 1980. This appeared to give substantial economy combined with higher maximum power output, and in the mid-1980s Wardale was in China, helping to redesign the standard 2-10-2 that was still being built there.

Another, even more radical, attempt to sustain the coal-burning locomotive was ACE 3000, a United States enterprise supported by the coal industry. This, scheduled for construction in the 1980s, was a condensing compound 4-8-2 with a cab in front. The fire was to be of gas-producer type, and combustion rates and other variables were to be microprocessor controlled. The ultimate fate of this project, expected to be twice as efficient as the conventional steam locomotive, was likely to depend on the comparative costs of coal and oil

As for the orthodox steam locomotive, this was still in regular service in many parts of the world in the late 1980s. Indeed, new steam locomotives were still being built in China, where steam traction was expected to continue into the twenty-first century, despite extending electrification and dieselization. The 'QJ' 2-10-2, a derivative of a Soviet Railways design, was still being produced by the Datong Works in 1987, while the Tangshan Works, restored after a disastrous earthquake, were producing a 2-8-2 steam locomotive.

In India, dieselization and electrification took their toll, and production of steam locomotives finished in the 1970s, although spare components continued to be produced. By the mid-1980s

Left: A French train in Savoy, running over steel and concrete crossties and hauled by a CC-7100-type electric locomotive.

Below left: A dual-current electric locomotive of Soviet Railways at a Finnish frontier station in 1979, having hauled a Leningrad to Helsinki train out of Russia.

Right: A sturdy 'TKt48'-type 2-8-2 tank locomotive, a postwar design still active in Poland, where it was designed and built.

Above left: An 'O3'-type Pacific leaves Halberstadt with a passenger train. Steam traction still survives in Eastern Germany for both passenger and freight work.

Left: One of the numerous Chinese Railways 'QJ'-type 2-10-2 locomotives working hard with a tank train. Two Chinese locomotive works are still constructing mainline steam locomotives.

Right: A German-built 0-8-0 in Turkey. This is one of the standard Prussian Railways 'G8' type, many of which were used in Turkey and central Europe. Although the Turkish railways imported many British locomotives, the predominant influence was German.

the older British-built types had largely disappeared and it was evident that steam traction would be confined to a handful of more modern designs. On the broad gauge these would be the 'WG' 2-8-2, a freight locomotive of British inspiration that had been mass produced at the new Chittaranjan Locomotive Works in the 1950s and 1960s, and the bullet-nosed 'WP' 4-6-2, designed in the United States and constructed in several countries. On the meter gauge it would again be postwar 'YG' 2-8-2 and 'YP' 4-6-2 classes that would survive the longest, although on both gauges American-built 2-8-2s, acquired during and after the war, were still active in the late-1980s.

Steam traction also remained important in parts of Africa. In the South African Republic diesel power was adopted at a pace which seemed irrational, given that country's dependence on oil imports and its abundance of coal. Steam traction was increasingly confined to certain areas and to certain classes of locomotive, of which the massive Class '25NC' 4-8-4 was very prominent. The Garratts were early casualties although, in common with other withdrawn designs, some of them were sold for use on colliery railways.

In Zimbabwe there was something of a steam renaissance. Imported diesels, producing extremely low productivity indices, thanks to spare parts shortage and lack of good maintenance facilities, proved inadequate and steam locomotives, sidetracked for scrap, were taken into works and restored to traffic; thus the Garratts of the former Rhodesian Railways gained a fresh lease of life, as they also did in neighboring Zambia. Farther north, in the Sudan, famine produced another implicit acknowledgment that the blandishments of the diesel salesmen should have been resisted more stoutly. When international aid produced the grain to relieve the famine of the southern Sudan it was found that the railways could not handle the traffic, for here too, the new diesel locomotives were failing, with 75 percent out of service. As this was an emergency situation, in which realities had priority over image-building, it was decided to renovate the steam locomotive

Left: Two 'WP' Pacifics of India's Western Railway at Baroda. Several hundred of these locomotives are at work all over India. Many were built there, but others were supplied by a variety of countries, often as part of economic aid schemes.

Below far left: The visible effect of using soft coal; South African Railways still makes use of steam traction, despite recent dieselization.

Below left: A British-built 2-6-0 of the Paraguayan Railways, still an all-steam operation. As in the Argentine, the front buffers are hinged safely back except when they are in use.

Left: A mixed train in the famine-stricken Sudan.

Right: The 'Red Devil,' a standard South African 4-8-4, rebuilt to incorporate the latest innovations in locomotive technology. Long trials were held; the rusty smokebox door, a result of overheating, suggests that the tests were taken to the limit. The knowledge gained was later used by the Chinese Railways.

Below: A 4-8-2 with a mixed train serving a South African township. This '19D' class of locomotive was built in the 1940s and with its light axle-weight is often used for branchline service.

fleet. A number of quite modern British-built 2-8-2 locomotives were sent to a works in South Wales for refurbishing, and other steam locomotives were repaired and returned to traffic by the Atbara works in Sudan itself. The units repaired in South Wales were also modernized with Lempor exhausts, after which their fuel costs were comparable to those of diesel locomotives.

In 1977 the DB in West Germany withdrew its last steam locomotives, having wisely kept steam traction alive in the years of large-scale electrification so as to avoid over production of diesels. British Railways had ended steam traction a decade before, and steam had also disappeared from French Railways. In Austria, Portugal and Italy steam hung on a little longer, but by the mid-1980s European steam traction was confined to Eastern Europe. Poland, in particular, still operated many steam services, although the end of steam traction was expected around 1990. The postwar Polish-built 'Tk48' 2-8-2 tank locomotive was likely to be the last class in service. In Yugoslavia, East Germany, and

Romania there were still pockets of steam operation; Romania even preserved on its books a few remaining veterans of the Prussian 'P38' 4-6-0 type. The USSR and Hungary also had a few steam locomotives in service, mainly for yard work and extra trains. The Turkish railways, meanwhile, repeatedly announced the forthcoming end of steam, but somehow steam traction survived there, having proved less dispensable than expected.

While regular steam traction had disappeared on North American railroads, in South America it still lingered on in the 1980s. Paraguay, which was too impoverished to modernize its railways, relied on British 2-6-0s, supplemented by second-hand locomotives bought from the Argentine. Bolivia and Peru had already adopted diesel power, and Chile was about to, but in the Argentine and Ecuador there were still regular steam-hauled services. Steam could also be found in Uruguay, while Brazil and the Argentine each had coal-hauling lines devoted entirely to steam traction.

The Passenger Train: Crisis and Survival

Despite growing car ownership, the railways in Western Europe, after some difficult years, succeeded in holding and even attracting passengers with vastly improved services and careful fare-setting. But in the United States and Canada, despite the efforts of some passenger-conscious companies, the passenger train remained such a loss-making proposition that the railroads were finally allowed to abandon the business altogether, being required only to make their tracks available for passenger trains operated by government-inspired and subsidized passenger train corporations, notably Amtrak in the United States and Via Rail in Canada.

Meanwhile, in both Europe and America, the responsibility for popular but loss-making suburban services was increasingly handed over to local authorities which, having learned that expensive highway construction brought more problems than it solved, were willing to make a financial contribution to enable peak-hour traffic to move by train rather than by automobile. Thus many city terminals were enlivened by trains, operated by the mainline railways, but painted in the liveries of the various local passenger authorities that sponsored and subsidized them.

In most of Western Europe, including Britain but not Ireland, the railways responded to difficulty by providing better services over their main lines, while neglecting or abandoning their secondary services. This effort to a large extent succeeded in not only holding, but developing, the passenger market. In Britain, for example, the railways began to derive most of their income from passengers, and not from freight, as previously.

In North America the picture was quite different, with freight revenue forming an ever-increasing proportion of the railroads' total income as passenger services declined. In the immediate postwar years, most United States railroads made a determined effort to rejuvenate their passenger services. New rolling stock was purchased which, hauled by cab-type diesels, could be plausibly described as streamlined. By 1948 the railroads were operating 250 such streamlined trains, and about 33 percent of the passengers benefitted from them; a proportion that would grow in subsequent years. Some new eye-catching trains were introduced. The *California Zephyr*, for example, operated jointly by the Burlington, Denver and Rio Grande, and Western Pacific railroads, was a stainless-steel train timed to allow passengers to enjoy the Feather River Canyon and other spectacular scenery. The *Lark* of the Southern Pacific provided a 12-hour overnight trip between San Francisco and Los Angeles. It was all-Pullman, and had a magnificent dining unit consisting of 3 cars with articulated suspension; but it needed no fewer than 21 members of crew, while carrying less than 2 bus-loads of passengers.

Novel rolling stock was also introduced. The first dome car, followed by many others, was introduced on the Burlington Railroad in 1945; passengers could climb into a glass-topped section above the car roof to look at the scenery. The Santa Fe Railroad soon went one better by providing what in effect were double-decker cars on its *El Capitan*; passengers sat on the glass-enclosed upper deck, leaving the lower deck for sleeping and other services. The Burlington Railroad was also the first to use the Slumbercoach. This enabled coach-class passengers to use sleeping accommodation, formerly the preserve of those buying first-class tickets. For a small supplement, they could use one of the tiny sleeping compartments of this vehicle which, ingeniously arranged, accommodated 40 passengers. Another success was the Budd car, or Rail Diesel Car (RDC), introduced in 1950. These self-propelled rail cars, came in 4 configurations and could run as single units or be coupled together to form trains. They reduced operating costs considerably and thereby enabled services to be maintained on secondary and branch lines.

Left: A narrow-gauge passenger train
in northern Austria. Dieselization
helped many rural passenger
services to survive in the difficult
postwar world.

Above: Commuters arriving at
Liverpool St Station, London,
in the 1970s.

Right: A London to South Wales
train in the 1950s. This is a typical
Western Region long-distance train
of the period, headed by a Great
Western 'Castle' class 4-cylinder
4-6-0.

Left: The *Red Arrow* overnight luxury Moscow to Leningrad train in 1957. Despite its name, it was painted blue.

Below left: The last *20th Century Limited* leaves Grand Central Station in 1967. Fluted stainless-steel exteriors were characteristic of postwar Pullman-built passenger cars.

Right: An Amtrak passenger train arriving in Washington DC, the southern terminal of the so-called North-Eastern Corridor from Boston and New York, Amtrak's busiest route.

Below right: The rear dome observation car of Via Rail's Vancouver to Montreal trans-continental train.

Left: One of Amtrak's lightly loaded services, the diesel-hauled Montreal to New York *Adirondack* pulls out of Montreal on formerly Canadian Pacific trackage. The rolling stock is part of an order placed by Amtrak soon after its establishment.

Above right: A TGV train ready to leave the Gare de Lyon in Paris.

Below right: When the Trans-European network was set up, the participating railways each designed their own trains. This is the German contribution, a high-powered diesel set, shown here at the Gare du Nord in Paris.

But the gap between costs and revenues widened. The final blow was the decision of the United States Post Office to transfer mail traffic from rail to highway whenever possible. The guaranteed mail contract had been a vital part of railroad passenger revenue and with its loss passenger deficits could only rise.

1967 was perhaps the beginning of the end. The Illinois Central and the Pennsylvania railroads added coaches to their hitherto all-Pullman *Panama Limited* and *Broadway Limited*, implicitly acknowledging that the airlines had scooped the market for the higher class of passenger. The Erie-Lackawanna Railroad's old-established *Phoebe Snow*, connecting New York with Chicago, was cut, while the pride of the NYC, the *Twentieth Century Limited*, disappeared from the timetables as the NYC announced that it intended to discontinue all its longer-distance trains.

The Frisco Railroad, meanwhile, became a freight-only railroad and by 1967 the proportion of railroad mileage carrying a passenger service fell to 32 percent, compared with 71 percent in 1947. In the next decade railroads presented a succession of 'train-off' petitions to the authorities, and by the mid-1970s it was evident, despite the continuing persistence of a few managements, that the long-distance passenger train was about to disappear from the American scene. To prevent this, in 1971 the federal government established Amtrak. This was to operate passenger trains over the tracks of the railroad companies, the latter receiving a fee and dropping their own surviving passenger trains. Over the years Amtrak developed its own image, and bought new rolling stock which included double-decker 'Superliner' cars for its western routes, where height restrictions were more generous. Its operations were divided between the North East Corridor route (Washington-New York-Boston), whose tracks it owned and reconstructed, and where the train service was frequent and profitable, and its other routes, which were a selection from the long-distance passenger network once offered by the railroads. As its losses were made up by government sub-

sidy, its choice of routes was changeable, being affected by the need to keep its deficit as low as possible and by the political pressures that could be placed on it to maintain services to one or another city. By the 1980s, some states had begun to pay Amtrak for the operation of intrastate trains. California, for example, subsidized a San Francisco to Los Angeles service.

In Canada Via Rail was set up to relieve the CN and CP of their long-distance passenger services. In the 1960s the CN had made a great effort to save its passenger services, offering fare reductions on off-peak days, complimentary meals for first-class passengers, and new trains such as the 'Rapidos' which, for example, reduced the Montreal to Toronto schedule to 5 hours for the 335 miles. These measures did attract passengers, but the increase was not enough to clear the deficit. Via Rail was less glamorous than Amtrak, and was obliged to soldier on with outdated equipment and to pay the 2 companies a high price for the use of their tracks and maintenance facilities. Its only leap forward, the purchase of a fleet of Canadian-built fast diesel trains, the LRC ('Light, Rapid, Comfortable'), came to grief when these trains proved to be victims of multiple design defects. Nevertheless, Via Rail did preserve passenger services on most of the main lines, including the transcontinental route through the Rockies.

Meanwhile, great things were happening on British Railways, which was anxious to dispel the old public image of grimy, slow, and overcrowded trains. A few diesel Pullman trains were operated in the 1960s, but these were overshadowed by the electrification from London to Birmingham, Liverpool, and Manchester, which permitted the introduction of a fast and frequent service, attracting far more new passengers than had been expected. With this encouragement, other plans were made. The term 'Inter-City' was adopted as a brand name intended to signify a better-than-usual service; as such, it was highly successful, with the German Railways copying it for their own new passenger service, and with its echo in the later 'Euro-City' marketing device.

International and High-Speed Trains

Because of the out-of-town situation of airports, city center to city center rail transit times are usually less than air transit up to distances of about 250 miles. Most European passenger journeys are shorter than this, so it has been the private automobile rather than the airliner that has been the main rival. To keep businessmen on the trains, the Western European railways introduced the TEE or Trans-Europ Express service; a network of extra-fare trains using ultra-modern equipment and providing the best possible and most reliable service. These operated both nationally and internationally, and acquired a high reputation but finally, in 1987, were replaced by the Euro-City network. Euro-City trains, operated by all the EEC countries plus Switzerland and Austria, are air-conditioned and have a minimum average speed of 56mph, except in mountainous regions.

Meanwhile, a handful of the traditional prewar international trains, including the long-lived *Nord Express*, soldiered on and were supplemented by a new concept, the auto-train, which carried both passengers and their cars, usually in a north-south direction. The auto-train also appeared in the United States, serving Florida.

The old *Orient Express* ceased to run, but its name was taken by a high-fare traditional luxury train for the tourist trade, operating between London and the Mediterranean. Another interesting international train was the *Catalan Talgo*. Operating between Madrid and Geneva, this took one of the unique Spanish 'Talgo' trains, with adjustable axles to suit the 2 gauges, into France and Switzerland.

The quest for higher speeds continued in Europe. At first it was the French *Mistral*, running over electrified lines from Paris to Marseilles, that held the main records, being scheduled to average 84mph over the 195 miles from Paris to Dijon. In 1954 the SNCF, in special trials with electric locomotives, reached a maximum speed of 151mph.

Unprecedented high speeds were reached in Japan on the New Tokaido Line, opened in 1964. This, later extended, was a standard-gauge route, unlike the other Japanese main lines, which are of 3-foot 6-inch gauge. Its trains could reach a maximum of 130mph, while averaging 112mph between Yokohama and Nagoya. The concept of building an entirely new railway for high-speed passenger trains was later adopted by the French for their TGV service. The first such route, from Paris to Lyons, began operations in 1981 with 13 daily trains capable of reaching 162mph and consequently providing the world's fastest average intercity speeds.

In Britain, there was a preference for running high-speed trains over existing track, despite the interference from other traffic and

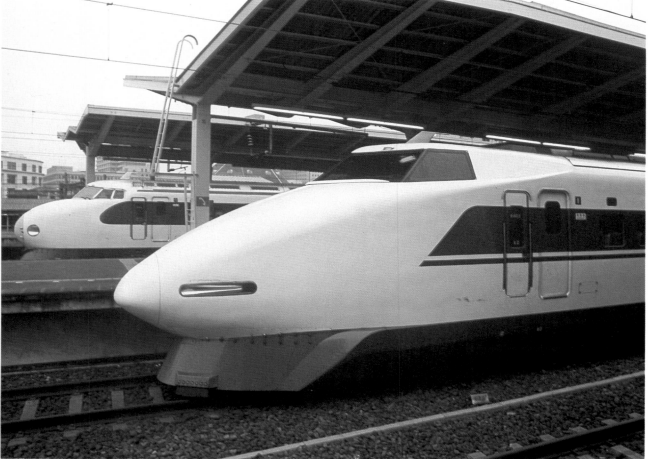

Above left: One of British Rail's HST services skirts the South Devon coast on the London to Plymouth line, which was the first to be served by these very successful trains.

Left: Trains of the Japanese Tokaido Line.

Above right: One of the XPT trains operating in Australia. These are modeled on the British HST and, although built in Australia, are not intended for very high speeds.

Right: The 'ET403,' a German semi-experimental train operated by German Federal Railways to provide a service from Düsseldorf to Frankfurt Airport.

the presence of relatively sharp curves. The diesel-powered HST, having a permanently attached locomotive at each end, went into service on the Western Region in 1976 and was an immediate success. Later additions to the fleet allowed the East Coast main line and the North-East to South-West trunk line to benefit from this innovation. Typically HST services averaged over 80mph, but in 1985 one of the Leeds to London trains reached 145mph and ran 100 miles at an average of 120mph.

A development of the concept, the Advanced Passenger Train, was abandoned after prolonged teething troubles had outlasted the nervous fortitude of the British Rail administration. A variant of the HST, however, was built in Australia: the XPT. This was an eventual success in New South Wales, despite a public opinion that resented the initial practice of charging first- and second-class passengers exactly the same fare and which took a long time to grasp that with their sharp curves, the New South Wales lines could not permit the high speeds that were associated with the HST in Britain.

Other countries also adopted the high-speed concept. The United States had been among the first of these, with the 'Metro-liner' trains between New York and Washington, introduced on the eve of Amtrak's establishment. These had been a mild dis-appointment, for the envisaged high average speeds were not quite reached. But Amtrak in the 1980s was investing heavily in its North East Corridor trackage, and 100mph schedules were becoming feasible. In Germany, a series of new high-speed rail-ways was being built, connecting with existing main lines. The South African Railways, never having had any high-speed pre-tensions, did half-heartedly introduce the *Metroblitz* train in 1984, which covered the 43-mile Johannesburg to Pretoria route in 44 minutes. It was withdrawn a year later on the grounds of poor patronage, but the true lesson was that radically new services, if they were to attract enough passengers to justify them, needed long advance planning and really sustained publicity. The British and French railways, in particular, had succeeded very well because they understood these requirements.

Above left: An exercise in nostalgia; a present-day tourists' Venice-Simplon 'Orient Express' passes through Austria.

Left: One of the Spanish National Railways many Talgo train services.

Above right: The *Blue Train* of South African Railways.

Right: An LRC train of Via Rail enters Montreal.

Piggyback, Kangaroos, and the Merry-go-round

Although the decline of 'smokestack' industries gave railways an added incentive to compensate for diminishing traditional bulk traffics like ore and coal by competing hard for merchandise shipments, many railways still thrived on heavy low-value freight. For example, in the USSR, whose railways carried as much freight as the railways of the rest of the world added together, trains carrying block loads of coal, ore and timber followed each other in endless succession at 10-minute intervals on the busier sections of line through the Urals.

The oil crises of the 1970s stimulated coal production in several parts of the world, with massive imports by some countries. Coal for Japan, for example, was shipped from Canada via the Canadian Pacific Railway and from Australia via the Queensland and New South Wales railway systems. In the United States, a few railroads benefitted from the shift of coal production to the less sulphurous resources of the West. The Burlington Northern, among others, introduced unit coal trains typically consisting of one hundred and ten 100-ton cars, with a payload of 11,000 tons.

In the United States, long trains were traditionally operated as a means of reducing wage costs. As they became longer and heavier, the strain on couplings and braking systems was sometimes relieved by placing some of the diesel units at the middle or toward the rear of the trains, with radio control from the leading locomotive unit. This practice was imitated in the USSR, so as to reduce the number of trains on congested lines. In South Africa, too, double-length unit trains were run from the coalfields of the Transvaal and Natal down to Richards Bay. Such trains, over a mile long, carried a payload of 10,000 tons and had 3 electric locomotives at the head and 5 more in the middle.

In Western Europe trains were much shorter. British Rail's heaviest regular train for many years was an iron-ore train of only 3300 gross tons. British Rail, however, did develop a technique for moving coal from pithead to power station. What were known as merry-go-round trains were used. These were unit trains which, with locomotives adapted for ultra-slow running, were loaded and unloaded while on the move. This eliminated terminal holdups and allowed the trains to attain high daily mileages, a prime requirement for low costs.

Britain did not adopt the 'piggyback' system for high-value merchandise. Known in North America as TOFC (trailer on flatcar), this placed road semitrailers on flatcars for the trunk component of their trip. The extra expense of carrying the trailers' running gear as well as their load-carrying body, plus height restrictions, excluded this technique from Britain. But in France and elsewhere in Europe, height restrictions were overcome by the 'Kangaroo' flatcar, which had an underfloor pouch to carry the trailers' wheels.

When TOFC was introduced in the 1950s it did not meet with the approval of all American railroads, for some considered the container more viable. This could be carried on a flatcar and transferred to and from a road truck for pickup and delivery, but needed expensive cranes at the railway terminals. The New York Central and a few other railroads adopted the 'Flexivan' container system but, being in a minority, were eventually driven to use piggyback.

However, in the last few years the container system, thanks to its adoption by shipping lines, has been accepted by many American railroads. Pacific shipping companies, led by the American President Lines, concluded that it was cheaper to tranship freight destined for the eastern United States at Pacific ports, rather than to take it by sea through the Panama Canal. The railroads could haul the lines' trains, with containers loaded 2-deep, from, say, Los Angeles to Chicago, at an average speed of over 40mph, which was competitive with highway truck schedules. In the mid-1980s such 'doublestack' trains typically carried 200

Left: A unique answer to the problem of finding a return load for specialized freight cars; a Peruvian flatcar adapted to carry lead ingots down to the docks at Callao and to return with oil fuel for the refineries.

Above right: Prototype containers for British 'Freightliner' trains on exhibition in 1964. Archaic 4-wheeler cars, as used by BR at that time, form the background.

Right: A Sealand 'Doublestack' container train.

Left: '10-Pack' container cars of the Santa Fe Railroad. The skeletal, lightweight, design of these cars is clearly evident.

Below: Although in many respects victims of the automobile, the railways do derive much traffic from the automobile-makers. These are Canadian National trilevel cars for carrying new automobiles from factory to distribution point. Other North American railroads use similar cars, but in Europe 3-deep loading is not possible.

Right: The Santa Fe Railroad carrying pipes for pipeline construction, another example of a railroad deriving traffic from a competitor.

containers, were approximately a mile long, and were hauled by 6 diesel units.

Piggyback continued to be used, and a number of railroads introduced fast services to handle it. Sometimes it was possible, too, to negotiate reduced crews for such trains. However, although container and piggyback traffic grew, it was not without problems, not the least of which was that it was often unprofitable because of the competitive rates the railroads had to offer. Technical expedients in the form of novel rolling stock were sometimes adopted to improve matters. The Southern Pacific's 'Ten-Pack,' for example, used skeletal flatcars weighing 11 tons per trailer, as against the 23 tons of conventional flatcars. Then there was the 'RoadRailer,' which after considerable travail was becoming a plausible proposition in the mid-1980s; this was a highway trailer with a set of railroad wheels that could be lowered for movement over the rails, the trailers being close-coupled to form a train.

In Britain, container trains were known as Freightliners and won considerable new traffic. However, for the same reasons as in the United States, they had difficulty in making a profit. By the mid-1980s, after the government had allowed highway operators to introduce the so-called 'juggernauts,' very large trailers, Freightliner services were regarded as viable propositions only when the length of haul was over 250 miles. Meanwhile, BR introduced a new fleet of air-braked freight cars with which it provided a network of regular 'Speedlink' conventional freight trains. Helped, on occasions, by government grants to companies installing rail tracks on their premises, BR also entered into long-term contracts with major industries which often provided their own specialized freight cars for regular trains linking their establishments. The oil companies, for example, sent regular trains of refined products from refineries to distribution points, and there was a growing traffic in roadstone, with companies despatching heavy trainloads of stone in their own or leased freight cars from quarries to the distribution depots. Also common, and not only in Britain, was the carriage of new automobiles from factory to distribution centers. Bilevel, and in the United States, trilevel, cars were provided for these services in which, paradoxically, the railroads had a marked cost advantage over any highway delivery.

In the postwar era railway freight services were transformed just as radically as passenger services, and a clear indication of this was the increasing use of specialized freight cars. The traditional United States boxcar, which could carry almost anything except perishables and liquids, although not very efficiently, began to lose its popularity, and the same phenomenon could be observed on other railroads. Another advance was the introduction, first in the United States, then in Britain, of a nationwide electronic information system (known as TOPS in Britain). This enabled railways to tell their clients exactly where shipments were, and when they would arrive. It also facilitated planning of freight car movements so that, while fewer would be needed, they would be more speedily available for loading. In Britain, this contributed to the radical improvement of freight car utilization, expressed by the fact that whereas traffic fell by around 25 percent between 1938 and 1983, the freight-car stock was reduced by as much as 90 percent.

Success on Shortlines

Almost all railroad traffic in the United States is handled by about 24 Class 1 railroads, but there have always been hundreds of shortline companies in operation. They are hard to count, because openings, closures, and mergers are almost a weekly occurrence, but in 1985 there were approximately 400 such lines. About 10 percent of these had more than 500 freight cars in service and, taken collectively, they were important both as feeders of freight traffic to the big railroads and as suppliers of transportation services to their local communities.

In recent decades, federal financial and technical assistance has been made available to selected shortlines. In 1980 the Staggers Rail Act, among other things, contained provisions for financial aid to independent feeder railroads and also relaxed the rate-making regulations for lines earning small revenues. After the Class 1 Rock Island and Milwaukee railroads became bankrupt, fresh measures were taken to make it easier for local interests to take over selected lines from moribund companies.

Because of their freedom from national work-rules, their lack of long-term debt, their local knowledge and connections, and, often, relief from local taxation, the shortlines could often achieve success where the original big railroads had failed. The states themselves sometimes took over lines, Vermont leading the way in 1963 by acquiring parts of the failing Rutland Railroad,

Above: An East German Mallet-type locomotive takes water at Alexisbad, on a busy narrow-gauge system in the Harz Mountains.

Left: An electric train of the Alpenzellerbahn, a meter-gauge local railway in Switzerland.

Right: Another, and quite extensive, meter-gauge Swiss railway, the Furka-Oberalpbahn. The electric locomotive is hauling a car-carrying train, an invaluable service in this area of snow and steep valleys.

Above left: A mixed train about to leave Gmünd, center of an extensive Austrian 2-foot 6-inch gauge system.

Left: A narrow-gauge train passes beneath a broad-gauge train near Baroda in western India.

Above right: Modernization of the Cuzco-Santa Ana Railway in Peru; a new Japanese-built diesel locomotive takes the morning train into the mountains.

which it converted into the short Vermont Central Railroad and Green Mountain Railroad. New York, subsequently, acquired the big commuter Long Island Railroad and Michigan the Ann Arbor Railroad, among others.

Although shortlines are not an exclusively American phenomenon, they are much less common elsewhere. In Britain, if the lines of industrial users are excluded on the grounds that they are not public railways, such lines barely exist, although in the past the 'light railway' would have fallen into that category. In Germany, Switzerland and Austria, however, small railways are numerous, and often more concerned with passengers than with freight. Topography has been a factor in these survivals, for in mountain regions a light or narrow-gauge railway could serve a

particular valley without needing a physical connection to a mainline railway. Many of these lines are electrified and provide frequent services for rural localities which often have substantial populations as well as scenic attractions to provide a tourist traffic. Occasionally, and notably in Austria, local railways may belong to the state railway but be operated independently.

Historically, narrow-gauge railways were usually built after the main lines, and were intended to provide cheap services for low-population areas. They should, therefore, have been early victims of rural truck and bus services. In many cases they were, especially in North America and western Europe, but some of them have survived not only in central Europe but more or less throughout the world. In Portugal, where many meter-gauge lines were built to supplement the 5-foot 6-inch gauge network, the narrow gauge is still flourishing, with new rolling stock and diesel locomotives. In India, there has been occasional regauging of meter-gauge trackage to 5 feet 6 inches, but in general the meter and narrower gauges remain intact.

Germany was once a country of numerous narrow-gauge lines, and France and Belgium had meter-gauge systems alongside the standard gauge. Most of these have disappeared in France and Belgium, but narrow-gauge lines survive in both East and West Germany, especially in East Germany, where steam traction is still used. Some of the East German lines have a tourist potential, but they also provide freight and passenger services for their localities.

Two-foot gauge lines in Natal are now closed, but there is talk of the resuscitation of 1 or 2 of them by local interests. The South African narrow gauge does survive in industrial uses, especially in the cane fields, as it does in Australia, Cuba, Indonesia and elsewhere. Moreover, South African Railways' lengthy 2-foot gauge Port Elizabeth to Avontuur line was still active in the mid-1980s.

In China, new narrow-gauge trackage is still being laid as an alternative to road-building. In 1986 there were about 2250 miles of local railways, and about 1500 miles of these were narrow gauge. Local railways of both gauges were to be extended, and the Chinese calculated that the cost of building a 2-foot 6-inch gauge line was only about 15 percent that of a standard-gauge railway.

In Britain, where public narrow-gauge railways were always rare, there still exist a number of lines kept open by preservation societies but, in addition, 2 old-established lines originally built for tourist traffic still flourish. One of these, the Vale of Rheidol line, once owned by the Cambrian Railway, then by the Great Western, is now the only British Rail line operated by steam traction. The other, not far away in North Wales, is the Snowdon Mountain Railway, operating steam rack-and-pinion locomotives up the mountainside. This railway has the unusual 2-foot 7½-inch gauge, as do some mountain lines in Switzerland.

Left: On the narrow gauge in eastern India. Such lines may carry an intensive commuter traffic, and sporadic closures by local governments have frequently led to vigorous, and sometimes successful, protest.

Above right: The *Apple Express*, a tourist train, run as a supplementary operation of the Port Elizabeth to Avontuur narrow-gauge line in South Africa.

Below right: One of the smart electrically hauled trains of the Zugspitzbahn in Bavaria. These derive most of their traffic from mountain walkers in summer and from skiers in winter.

Preserving the Railroad

In the 1980s, each year, scores of special steam trains were operated over British Rail, most of them sponsored by BR but with a fair proportion organized by a consortium of private locomotive-owners. With its numerous preservation schemes, tourist railways, and museums, Britain clearly led the world in the railway preservation movement.

The involvement of British Rail in operating profitable vintage trains contrasted with its attitude of the 1960s, when it was determined to obliterate reminders of the steam age. By the mid-1980s, as well as accepting the operation by others of one-off steam excursions, it was running regular summer-only steam trains on several routes, with its 'Shakespeare Limited,' a Sunday dining car service from London to Stratford-on-Avon, attracting a high proportion of overseas tourists, and its York to Scarborough and Fort William to Mallaig services interesting a more domestic public. Other routes were opened from time to time; in 1986 a steam service was tentatively introduced from Salisbury, and in the following year on the Central Wales line to Barmouth.

Other excursions were frequently operated with locomotives based on the privately owned Carnforth locomotive depot in Cumbria; one series of steam excursions, a publicity run sponsored by British Nuclear Fuels to take passengers to look at the Windscale processing plant, caused controversy.

Despite its initial reluctance to run preserved steam lines, the extent of BR's participation in steam excursions was quite unusual compared to other countries. In Germany the DB long resisted steam excursions, relenting only after the 150th anniversary celebrations of German railways showed that running steam trains did not lead the public to suppose that railways remained in the steam age. In the United States, some railroad managements (more often, their presidents) showed noticeable enthusiasm for such excursions; in the mid-1980s the Norfolk Southern Railroad was distinguishing itself with steam excursions over its very extensive network, using 2 former Norfolk and Western locomotives, the 4-8-4 No 611 and a resuscitated Mallet, No 1218. Other frequent performers on United States mainline railroads were a Union Pacific 4-8-4, No 8444, a Nickel Plate Railroad 2-8-4 of the 'Superpower' generation, a 'Superpower' 2-10-4 of the Texas and Pacific and a 4-6-2 of the Louisville and Nashville Railroad. One of the famous 'K4' 4-6-2s of the Pennsylvania Railroad, having stood on a plinth for many years, was returned to traffic in 1987. In Canada the Canadian National was also hospitable to steam excursions, whereas the Canadian Pacific was less so. A 'Royal Hudson' 4-6-4 of the latter company, however, hauled excursions out of Vancouver on the British Columbia Railway.

Left: A tourist train of the Cumbres and Toltec Railroad in New Mexico, a resurrected 3-foot-gauge line.

Right: Inside the Baltimore and Ohio Transportation Museum in Baltimore, which is mainly, but not entirely, devoted to relics of the Baltimore and Ohio Railroad.

Below right: A train of the Strasburg Railroad at Lancaster, Pennsylvania. This is a very successful tourist line, which preserves some of the atmosphere of the Pennsylvania Railroad.

Left: On the North Yorkshire Moors Railway, one of the most interesting of British preserved lines. The picture shows a 2-6-0 of the former LNER hauling vintage Pullman vehicles.

Right: Preserved Belgian Railways No 29013, one of a series of 2-8-0 locomotives supplied by Canada in 1945 to help resurrect the war-ravaged railway system.

Below right: One of the cool-season picnic trains operated by the Hotham Valley Tourist Railway in Western Australia.

Left: A tank car which once supplied London with milk from Devon and is now preserved by the Great Western Society at Didcot, near Oxford.

Below left: Some continental European locomotives have been imported for preservation in Britain. This is one of them, a representative of the celebrated compound 4-6-0 locomotives of the French Nord Railway.

Right: A former Prussian Railways 0-6-0 tank locomotive heads a tourist train on the Wutachtalbahn in West Germany.

In Australia it was enthusiast organizations which sponsored steam excursions, and the same situation existed in South Africa. Australian railways did, however, assemble 'vintage trains' of the old equipment which they despatched under steam to various local celebrations, typically to towns celebrating their centenaries. In New Zealand, the *Kingston Flyer* was one of the earliest railway-sponsored regular steam excursions. Another regular steam excursion was in Malaysia, where there was a Kuala Lumpur to Batu Caves service, which was sponsored by the local Kentucky Fried Chicken organization.

The running of mainline steam excursions was only one facet of the railway preservation movement. The acquisition and rehabilitation of old abandoned railways, and the establishment of railway museums, were the 2 other main activities. The steam locomotive was usually the inspiration of these enterprises, but vintage rolling stock, signaling equipment, and smaller items were also carefully preserved. As the years passed, old electric and diesel locomotives also began to feature.

The earliest of the enthusiast-preserved lines was the narrow-gauge Talyllyn Railway in Wales, reopened as a preserved line in the early 1950s. Other preserved railways were subsequently established in this area, including the Ffestiniog Railway with its unique 'Fairlie' locomotives. Reopening of standard-gauge lines began with the Bluebell Railway in Sussex in 1960, which prospered and amassed a wide range of locomotives. Its success inspired many other preservation projects, and there is a long and growing list of such railways in Britain. Among the older-established and larger projects are the Severn Valley in Shropshire, the Keighley and Worth Valley in Yorkshire, the Torbay and Dartmouth, and the North Yorkshire Moors railways. Most of these lines specialize, frequently reflecting the past railway age of their particular localities. For example, the Torbay and Dart-mouth reconstructs the traditional Great Western branch line, while the Great Central runs its trains over a former main line of the old Great Central Railway. The Nene Valley Railway at Peterborough, however, operates overseas items.

The railroad preservation scene in the United States is a little more volatile, with quite a few lines ceasing operation after a few unprofitable years. Successful railway preservation schemes require either a wealthy sponsor or a willing band of volunteer labor. With the less-concentrated United States population, it is sometimes difficult to assemble sizable groups of railroad enthusiasts within easy reach of a project. Nor do the American lines enjoy the government-sponsored employment schemes that sometimes make a temporary workforce available to British lines. On the other hand, because of the tourist attractions they offer, some preservation schemes have been initiated by state governments. West Virginia created a combined museum and active railroad from the remains of a logging enterprise at Cass, and recently Texas has opened a state-preserved railway.

The combination of a museum and active steam operations is also offered by Steamtown, near Scranton in Pennsylvania, and by the 2-foot gauge Edaville Railroad in Massachusetts, while the long-established Strasburg Railroad is adjacent to the Pennsylvania Railroad Museum.

Among other preserved lines with many years of operation is the Silverton Railroad, providing a steam run over one of the 3-foot gauge lines once owned by the Denver and Rio Grande Western Railroad. Also in the Rockies, at Chama in New Mexico, there is another 3-foot gauge line, the Cumbres and Toltec Scenic. In Canada, the Prairie Dog Central has for many years been offering trips out of Winnipeg behind a former CP Railroad 4-4-0 locomotive.

Despite a strong railway enthusiast movement, there are no

Left: Railway societies have established museums in all the Australian states. This one is at Williamstown, Melbourne, and is devoted mainly to the Victorian Railways. The 3 locomotives shown here are British designs, introduced in the 1880s.

Right: On the Bluebell Railway, a pioneering British preserved line and now flourishing.

preserved steam lines in South Africa. The situation is different, however, in Australia, where the narrow-gauge Puffing Billy Railway near Melbourne, and the Hotham Valley Railway, near Perth, to mention just 2, have been flourishing for several years. The Hotham Valley not only runs trains on its own lines but, on occasions, has provided locomotives for mainline steam trains. Mainline steam excursions are operated in all the eastern states.

Shortage of steam locomotives has sometimes been a limiting factor in the establishment of preserved lines. In Britain, luckily, after the quite rapid end of steam traction, withdrawn locomotives remained several years in a scrapyard at Barry, South Wales, giving time for preservation societies to raise the money for buying selected units for restoration. In the United States, purchases by individuals and the preservation by railroad companies of a few locomotives have provided most of the traction power. In France, because steam was scrapped before enthusiasts had quite realized the possibilities open to them, there has been a scarcity of steam locomotives that can be restored.

Several preservation societies have imported locomotives; the narrow-gauge Welshpool and Llanfair has 2 locomotives from remote former British colonies, and in the mid-1980s both the

Polish and Soviet railways were quoting fixed prices for their withdrawn steam locomotives.

Large-scale railway museums preceded the end of steam. The present-day National Railway Museum at York in Britain has its origins in a more modest York Railway Museum of the inter-war years. One of the best American museums, the Baltimore and Ohio Railroad Museum in Baltimore, also has a long history, as does the Transport Museum at Lucerne in Switzerland. More recent museums include the Railroad Museum at St Louis in the United States and the Canadian Railway Museum near Montreal. France has its Mulhouse Railway Museum, while exhibits in Germany are scattered through several museums. Surprisingly, neither the USSR nor South Africa yet possess museums exhibiting full-size locomotives and rolling stock, but in Australia there are several, each covering a particular state. The fear that the very existence of railway museums would perpetuate the alleged public belief that railways are anachronistic seems to have vanished. Modern railways are clearly different from those of a few decades ago, and in the mid-1980s there were, after all, about 9000 miles of new railway under construction in various parts of the world.

INDEX

Acknowledgments

The publisher would like to thank
the following people who helped in
the preparation of this book: David
Eldred, who designed it; Tanya
Hines, who edited it; Mandy Little,
who carried out the picture research;
and Ron Watson, who compiled the
index. Our thanks, too, to the
following picture agencies,
institutions and individuals for
supplying illustrations on the pages
noted:

Albany Institute: page 31(top)
Alco Historic Photographs: page
96(bottom)
Association of American Railroads:
pages 9(bottom), 15(top), 27(both),
32(top), 80(bottom), 82(bottom)
Bison Picture Library: pages
15(bottom), 32(bottom), 35(top),
42(top), 96(bottom)
BBC Hulton Picture Library: pages
8(bottom), 11(top), 14, 18(top),
20(both), 21(bottom), 29(both),
30(bottom), 48, 50(bottom), 51(both),
58(bottom), 66, 67(both), 70(both
both), 72(top), 73(bottom), 76(top),
95(top), 100-1, 101(top), 102(bottom),
106, 107(bottom), 108, 109(bottom),
112(bottom), 115, 118, 119(both), 120,
124, 129, 131(bottom), 132(top),
139(both), 152(top), 156(both)
BBC Hulton/Bettmann Archive:
pages 17, 58(top), 59(both), 61(top
both), 62, 64-5, 94 (bottom)
Phil Belbin: page 75(bottom)

Borough of Darlington Museum:
pages 12-13
Bridgeman Art Library: page
18(bottom)
Burlington Northern Railroad: pages
71(bottom left), 138
California State Railroad Museum:
page 130(bottom)
Canadian Pacific Rail Corporate
Archive: page 79(bottom)
East Sussex County Library: page
94(bottom)
Colin Garratt: pages 58, 128, 130,
135(bottom), 172(bottom), 173,
174(bottom), 176, 196
General Motors/Electro Motors
Division: pages 144(bottom),
145(both)
George Gloff © 1974 Kalmbach
Publications: page 164(bottom)
Hotham Valley Tourist Railway:
page 201(bottom)
Japanese Tourist Organisation: page
184(bottom)
Mrs V Johnstone/Battye Library:
page 49(bottom)
Ironbridge Gorge Museum: pages
16(top), 35(bottom), 63
Imperial War Museum, London:
pages 104, 104-5, 105
India Office: page 50(top)
Kalmbach Publishing Co. Collection:
pages 162(bottom), 163(top),
189(bottom), 198, 199(top)
Keystone Collection: pages
62-3(bottom), 98-9, 102(top),
109(top), 116, 143, 147(bottom),
149(bottom), 150-1, 153, 156(top),
167, 179(top), 189(top)

La Vie Du Rail: pages 41(top),
43(bottom), 93, 157(top),
166(bottom), 183(bottom)
Library of Congress: pages 40,
60-1(bottom)
Mansell Collection: pages 8(top), 10,
11(bottom), 19(top), 34(both), 54(top
& left), 69, 75(top both)
Museum of London: page 149(top)
National Railway Museum: pages
6-7, 9(top), 22(bottom), 28, 36-7,
42(bottom), 42-3, 49(top), 55(top
right), 60(top), 73(top), 74, 81(top),
85(both), 107(top), 125(top)
Peter Newark's Western Americana:
pages 16(bottom), 21(top), 22(top),
30(top), 33(top), 41(bottom), 46-7,
62-3(top), 65(top), 68(both), 71(top &
bottom right), 114(top), 117(bottom),
131(bottom), 146(top), 147(top), 154,
155(both)
Newberry Library: page 23(top)
New York Historical Society: page
31(bottom)
Norfolk Southern Corporation: pages
38(both), 39(both)
Leon Oberg: pages 81(bottom),
90(top), 141(top), 158(top), 185(top),
204
Osterreiche Gallery: page 52-3
PHMC Railroad Museum of
Pennsylvania: page 76
Santa Fe Railroad: pages 190(top),
191
Science Museum, London: page 54-5
W A Sharman: page 200
Smithsonian Institution: page
94(top)
SNCF/French Railways: page 170

South African Transport Services:
pages 57(bottom), 91(bottom), 103,
124(bottom), 160(bottom), 165(top),
177(both), 187(top), 197(top)
Brian Stephenson: pages 23(bottom),
45, 92, 122-3(bottom), 137(top),
158(bottom), 159, 168, 184(top),
185(bottom), 186(bottom),
192(bottom), 193, 201(top),
202(bottom), 203, 205
John Massey Stewart: page 80(top)
Union Pacific Railroad Collection:
page 70(top)
UPI/Bettmann: page 180(bottom)
Venice-Simplon-Orient Express:
page 186(top)
Bill Yenne: pages 18(bottom),
77(bottom), 78(bottom), 79(top),
112-3
John Westwood: pages 44, 82(top),
83(both), 84(both), 86, 86-7, 87,
88(both), 89, 90(bottom), 91(top),
97(both), 114(bottom), 117(top), 121,
122-3(top), 126-7(both), 132(bottom),
133, 134(both), 135(top), 136(bottom),
137(bottom), 140(both), 141(bottom),
142(both), 144(top), 146(bottom),
148(both), 152(bottom), 155(bottom),
157(bottom), 160(bottom), 161(both),
162(top), 165(bottom), 169(both),
170(bottom), 171(bottom), 172(top),
174(top), 175(bottom), 178,
179(bottom), 180(top), 181(both), 182,
183(top), 187(bottom), 188,
190(bottom), 192(top), 194(both), 195,
197(top), 199(bottom), 202(top)